UNSETTLING AUSTRALIA

READINGS IN AUSTRALIAN CULTURAL HISTORY

UNSETTLING AUSTRALIA

READINGS IN AUSTRALIAN CULTURAL HISTORY

LARS JENSEN

ATLANTIC
PUBLISHERS & DISTRIBUTORS

Published by

ATLANTIC
PUBLISHERS & DISTRIBUTORS
B-2, Vishal Enclave, Opp. Rajouri Garden,
New Delhi-110027
Phones : 25413460, 25429987, 25466842

Sales Office
7/22, Ansari Road, Darya Ganj,
New Delhi-110002
Phones : 23273880, 23275880, 23280451
Fax : 91-11-23285873
web : www.atlanticbooks.com
e-mail : info@atlanticbooks.com

ISBN 81-269-0406-2

Printed in India
at Nice Printing Press, Delhi

Preface

It is proof of the power wielded by nationalism that I have found it necessary to begin a book on Australian cultural history[1] by speaking of my own position in relation to studies of Australian culture, simply because I am not Australian, let alone Danish-Australian. The frequent conflation in nationalist discourse between reality/experience and representation, as if they are bound up inside a fully contained self-referential universe, has struck many academics intervening into debates on the constitution of particular national identities other than their own. The closer one cuts to the bone, the sharper the nationalist reaction; the more iconic the particular nationalistic representation has been in a particular national culture, the more jealously it has been guarded by what may be termed the national Establishment, which includes widespread academic circles. This is not, then, a particularly Australian phenomenon, but it is given a particular shape in an Australian context. Here the largest nationalist bone of contention has been the struggle over the Anzac legacy, which is conventionally regarded (and jealously guarded) as the stamping ground of Australian scholars. As we rapidly approach the centenary after the event which gave birth to the most cherished Australian nationalist myth[2],

1. I use the term 'Australian cultural history' here instead of 'Australian cultural studies', because I wish to make a distinction between on the one hand the discussion of particular themes and experiences regarded as characteristic of Australian culture, and historically arrived at, and on the other hand 'Australian cultural studies' referring to the different schools both interdisciplinary and traditional which are engaged in defining Australian cultural history.
2. The use of the term 'myth' here is not meant to be understood in the literary sense of fantasy, nor in the traditional anthropological sense, but in a sociological conception of the term as 'a collective belief that is built up in response to the wishes of the group rather than an analysis of the basis of the wishes'. [*The Macquarie Dictionary*, Macquarie University, 1991, p. 1178, (def. 5)].

the 'outsiders' intervening into the debate on its derived meanings, are still regarded with suspicion, regardless of their investment in Australian cultural studies, as if their schooling is somehow incomplete. If one regards schooling as being trained in the nation's ethos, then, of course, such a criticism does have a point. The criticism (rather than critique) of Bruce Kapferer's intervention into the debate on the creation of a national Australian identity through the construction of a nationalistic Anzac myth is one of the more familiar examples.[3]

My view of my own position is that of a European outsider with the privilege of having gained insight into Australian culture through my own preoccupation with Australian literature, history, popular culture and art for more than a decade. I could also argue for my numerous visits to Australia and lengthy stays, but have become increasingly wary of what precisely such statements are supposed to legitimate. My view here derives partly from Benedict Anderson's insightful arguments about the strength of nationalism's hold over the interpretation of 'national' histories, and in particular his emphasis on Ernest Renan's observation that forgetting is as important as remembering is for the nation.[4] In the case of the Anzacs, the Kelly story, the Eureka Stockade and other 'nation-building events' this highly specific process is expressed in the authorisation of selective representation, through the act of granting preference to certain versions of events over others. This narrativisation of selective history is helped as much by a process of selective forgetting as it is by selective remembering.

In certain ways the current study may be said to take its cue from the nation's process of forgetting. It begins with an insistence on the built-in limitations of focusing exclusively on the dominant stories as those, which have somehow survived

3. I return to this criticism in a later chapter, but the details can be found in Bruce Kapferer's introduction to the 1998 paperback edition of his *Legends of People, Myths of State* (London: Smithsonian Institute Press, 1998).
4. Benedict Anderson, *Imagined Communities* (London: Verso, 1991), p. 6 and pp. 199-201.

and therefore define the evolving nation-state.[5] Although part of the project of challenging dominant representations of the nation's space is to lay bare the power formations which generates this discourse, to merely do this is to accept the discursive ground defined by the same dominant nationalist representations. It is, therefore, also (and even more) important to uncover other cultural-historical processes of producing meaning, which have been deliberately displaced in the process of privileging certain narratives about the nation over others. The present study discusses that which predominant nationalist readings of Australian cultural history seek to repress. It focuses specifically on what may be described as the nation's most significantly internalised and externalised others, both understood in their ontological capacities as Aborigines and Asians[6], and as discursive categories. But it is equally important to stress that the study is also, and even precisely, about dominant themes in Australian culture, even if this book will not focus on the usual suspects when trying to identify how Australian cultural identities have been given shape.

My reading of Australian cultural history is influenced by a number of studies and collections of essays dealing with questions of national identity and the construction of meaning. However, there is an important point where I find my conceptualisation to be significantly different. Academic books on Australian cultural history are written with an Australian audience in mind, with a particular set of reference points that are readily recognisable to Australian scholars and students, but which also take for granted what constitutes an Australian

5. What I am suggesting here is that the struggle over particular versions of the past is a displaced struggle over contemporary meanings of national identity. 'Standing the test of time' becomes entangled with the reproduction of dominant narratives of the nation's evolution.
6. Both 'Aborigines' and 'Asians' are notoriously problematic terms, for they both have a history of lumping together quite disparate peoples spread throughout Australia and Asia. They have, as I will argue in the Introduction, a particular representational history in Australia, which is inseparable from their function in relation to the history of Australian nationalism.

experience. Such an approach makes certain positions more legitimate than others. I choose my words carefully here, for I am not governed by a desire to seek to dismiss prevalent readings of Australian cultural identities. Yet I am pursuing an approach that critically investigates how prevailing ways of seeing Australian culture cloud over other ways of seeing, and how they become in fact consensus manufacturing, anxiety driven models of identification which are aimed at overriding other disturbing concerns and presences.

My approach may be characterised as that of an informed outsider's perspective. I intend to implement this perspective by combining a general introduction to contemporary preoccupations in Australian culture with an attempt to single out what lies behind these themes, in order to generate a critical and insightful representation of Australian culture. Although I have, of course, been guided by a certain degree of infatuation with Australian culture, I remain a self-conscious outsider, which I believe gives me the benefit of examining critically those parts of Australian culture that become extremely difficult to write critically about as an Australian. Simply because of the difficulty of putting into perspective those shaping events that are closest to home.

LARS JENSEN

Table of Contents

Preface *v*

Introduction: Mapping the Territory 1

1. Infinite Rehearsals: Historiography and Australian Beginnings 30

2. Towards an Aboriginal-Asian Colonial Contact History 60

3. Geographic Dislocation: From European Satellite to Asian Backwater? 98

4. Multiculturalism and the Chinese-Australians 135

Conclusion 157

Introduction: Mapping the Territory

When Richard White published his seminal study of Australia's cultural history, *Inventing Australia*, in 1981, he initiated what was to become a whole series of books that deals with Australian culture from a range of different perspectives, from media representations, over historiographically based studies, to more sociologically orientated surveys. These publications include, in chronological order, Graeme Turner, *National Fictions* (1986); Fiske, Hodge and Turner, *Myths of Oz; Reading Australian Popular Culture* (1987); Castles, Kalantzis, Cope and Morrissey, *Mistaken Identity; Multiculturalism and the Demise of Nationalism in Australia* (1988); Bob Hodge and Vijay Mishra, *Dark Side of the Dream: Australian Literature and the Postcolonial Mind* (1991); John Frow and Meaghan Morris, *Australian Cultural Studies* (1993); Graeme Turner, *Making It National* (1994); Tom Griffiths, *Hunters and Collectors* (1996) and Wayne Hudson and Geoffrey Bolton (eds.), *Creating Australia; Changing Australian History* (1997). The list is far from exhaustive, but the works mentioned represent major contributions from a long list of interdisciplinary approaches.

Starting points

In the light of the profusion of studies on Australian cultural history a new departure for understanding Australian cultural identifications must necessarily begin with an examination of the existing genealogy of cultural history books, to understand how their preoccupations are arrived at as central concerns.

One of the interesting features of Australian cultural studies is that its practitioners seem to prefer to establish their own understanding and only indirectly draw attention to other studies and approaches in the area, let alone enter into a discussion with these, or their premises. As Meaghan Morris perceptively argues the 'real problem may be that the genre in which "histories" are being invented for cultural studies often leads people into positing a *single origin* for their practice'.[7] In a similar vein Jon Stratton and Ien Ang have suggested that Australian cultural studies traditionally has been modelled on British cultural studies[8], and as such is seen to have evolved from the Birmingham School. Yet, while it is fair to say that the conceptualisation, which informs cultural studies in Australia, has derived its inspiration from the Birmingham School, it is equally important to remember that Australian cultural critics draw attention to the uniqueness of the Australian experience.

Furthermore, the traffic of cultural theory between Britain to Australia has not been headed in one direction. Australian critics such as Graeme Turner and Meaghan Morris, have intervened both in the cultural theory debate in the Australian context, but also in the wider discourse on the origins of theoretical positions within cultural studies. The acceptance of the influence of particularly the Birmingham School owes much to what Australian cultural studies readers have found to be theoretically enabling for their own practice. Stratton and Ang identify this enabling influence as follows:

> Hall, Williams and Hoggart worked on a cultural studies in Britain which articulated a redefinition of culture by breaking down, in theoretical terms, the equation of the dominant culture with culture *per se*, opening up the terrain of the cultural for struggle, negotiation, and resistance.... The energizing impulse of British cultural studies has historically precisely lain in this critical concern with, and validation of, the subordinate, the marginalized, the subaltern within Britain.[9]

---

7. Meaghan Morris, 'On the Beach', in Lawrence Grossberg, Cary Nelson and Paula Treichler (eds) *Cultural Studies* (London: Longman, 1992), p. 455.
8. Stratton and Ang in Stuart Hall: *Critical Dialogues in Cultural Studies*, ed. by David Morley and Kuan-Hsing Chen (London: Routledge, 1996), p. 368.
9. Stratton and Ang in *Critical Dialogues*, p. 376.

The critical domain of the British school has been enabling for example for an Australian cultural studies critique that targets nationalistic representations as monocultural, exclusivist even chauvinistic. Graeme Turner takes up precisely this point when he relates the theoretical field of cultural studies to the Australian context:

> White Australian histories — as distinct from imperial or colonial histories — have, in a sense, *always* been histories 'from below': accounts of a subordinated (that is, a colonised) people, and of their construction of social groups and identities within an extremely repressive and authoritarian social and administrative structure...a history from below made British cultural studies relevant to Australians...from an Australian standpoint this general theoretical principle made it possible to foreground 'Australia' itself as marginal against a dominant 'Britain'.[10]

The convenient (negative) positioning of the British as oppositional to the (positive) emergence of an Australian subaltern perspective is rightly problematised by Stratton and Ang, who argue that 'in foregrounding Australia's subordinate status *vis-à-vis* Britain, [Turner's position entails]...its own silences and limited horizons'.[11] Instead Stratton and Ang present a diasporic model for interrogating Australian cultural history to escape the imperialist/nationalist bind that has continued to haunt approaches to Australian cultural studies. This diasporic model:

> which arguably would foreground issues related to Australia's history of non-Anglo immigration, the politics of multiculturalism and its impact on Australian national identity — would usefully complement and complicate Turner's postcolonial project and its preoccupation with the heritage of British colonialism for the construction of 'Australia'.[12]

10. Turner quoted by Stratton and Ang in *Critical Dialogues*, p. 377.
11. Stratton and Ang in *Critical Dialogues*, p. 377.
12. Stratton and Ang in *Critical Dialogues*, p. 384. Although this is not the place to discuss this issue, I find it important to dismiss Stratton and Ang's misunderstood use of the term 'postcolonial', which seems to rest on a simplistic notion of equating postcolonial with nationalistic anti-imperialism.

Yet if I share Ang and Stratton's view that other histories need to be included if nationalist readings of Australian cultural history are to be questioned, I find their provisional conclusion as to what such a 'new' cultural studies practice should ideally involve somewhat tame. Hence they speak of making 'the most of the provisionalness of constant renegotiation and re-articulation which has been heralded as one of the hallmarks of cultural studies'.[13] What I find particularly limiting in this approach is first of all that it speaks of an atemporal situatedness that does not take into account the 'white Australian' history in Australia, which has not only historically shaped 'white Australia's' relations with Asia/ns and Aborigines, but continues to inform perceptions of Australia's cultural identity, quite often with the aid of racially sanitised versions of Australia's cultural history. I find a post-colonial approach more enabling, because, while taking point of departure in the present, it reconnects the critique to the historical processes through which patterns of relations between white Australians on the one side and Asia/ns and Aborigines on the other, were established. Instead of seeking to bypass the unpleasantness of Australia's race-obsessed history it works through this history because of the realisation that these racially rooted relations continue to inform the conditions under which present-day relationships are negotiated. As such, it is pivotal to grasp the historical process in order to reach an understanding of the intercultural relations operating in Australia today.

In *Australian Cultural Studies: A Reader*[14] John Frow and Meaghan Morris in their Introduction also take point of departure in the Birmingham School as a way of grounding their own critical practice. But where Ang and Stratton use the term 'diaspora' in a relational discourse that constitutes the theoretical apparatus behind an operational multicultural practice, Frow and Morris draw attention precisely to the drawbacks of multiculturalism, and to the consensus seeking

13. Stratton and Ang in *Critical Dialogues*, p. 385.

14. *Australian Cultural Studies: A Reader* ed. by John Frow and Meaghan Morris (Chicago: University of Illinois Press, 1993).

anxieties which inform it.[15] Hence Frow and Morris question 'those totalising notions of culture which assume that there is always, at the end of cultural processes, the achievement of a whole and coherent "society" or "community"'.[16] Their criticism operates on two levels. First of all it is a critique of the already assumed progressiveness of the nation and the shadow side of this idea, modernity. Secondly, their criticism is levelled at multiculturalism as an instrument of the nation, here disguised as a progressive state. The limitation of such a multicultural practice is exposed in the following observation:

> it is always possible for the category of culture with which [the policy of multiculturalism] operates to remain at the decorative level of folkloric ethnic markers detached from substructures of real and agonistic difference; conversely, it tends to reproduce imaginary identities at the level of the ethnic 'community' and thereby to screen differentiations and contradictions *within* the community (those of class and gender, for example); it depends upon covering over an asymmetry between migrant and indigenous groups...and...on a final moment of absorption of difference back into unity at the level of language and national identity.[17]

What I find interesting about Frow and Morris's argument is that it is in fact less directed at multicultural practice itself (whose limitations are fairly evident to anyone who has followed the debate over its merits and shortcoming over the last couple of decades), and more at the theoretical platform that informs it. That theoretical platform is itself governed by a liberalist ideology about the progressive modernity of the nation(-state). Hence one project that grows out of this criticism is the questioning of the assumptions which inform modernity

---

15. It is arguable that the drawbacks have less to do with multiculturalism *per se*, which may be characterised as a practice that can be informed by all kinds of ideologically determined considerations. As such Howard's reluctance to actually say the 'm' word may ironically have less to do with its potentially challenging nature, and more with his failure to understand its potential as a conservative control mechanism.
16. *Australian Cultural Studies*, p. ix.
17. *Australian Cultural Studies*, p. ix.

and how that operates in an Australian context. This becomes a critique that questions the perceived nexus between demographic change and cultural change, as well as the nexus between liberalism and 'real', as opposed to 'cosmetic', tolerance.

The other project is similar in its intention to expose the repressive nature of nationalism, but does so by asking what happens when focus is shifted away from consensus experience to the marginalised. This approach is parallel in its assumptions to Frow and Morris's idea of 'covering over an asymmetry', but posits this asymmetry between a nationalist Anglo-Irish derived culture on the one side and other migrants and Aborigines on the other. The problem embedded in the asymmetry is not only an ethnicity based, monolithic categorising that is conservative and based on a principle of containment. It is also that the categorising grows out of a displacement rhetoric of belonging/unbelonging, where 'belonging' to the British-Irish stratum can also enshrine Australianness, whereas belonging to the Asian community is the only representation made available to the 'Asian', and as such it is this that simultaneously enshrines their unbelonging, their essential 'unaustralianness'. My critique is less based on showing the rather obvious shortcomings of multiculturalism, which many critics seem unable to distinguish from the multicultural moment in Australian history, and more to show how multiculturalism fails through the displaced containment strategy operated through a nationalist discourse.[18]

On the other hand I also wish to show how what may be termed 'Asian agency' articulates through the trope of 'difference' a voice that cannot be contained, and actively undermines a limited form of multiculturalism circumscribed by Anglo-Irish Australian domination. These voices also question received understandings of Australian cultural history, here defined in a very broad sense as paired off representations

18. Other critics talks about 'settler discourse' rather than 'nationalist discourse'. My preference for the latter term is due to my overriding concern not to single out settler discourse as a more legitimate national practice than migrant discourse.

and experiences that produce Australia as a nation for itself. It is important to recognise that the bound sets of representations need not necessarily be seen as a positive drive for coherent or cohesive national unity. Homogenisation can be driven by the fear of what is constructed as divisive strategies, and as such the underlying strategy is less aimed at the positive identification of the nation as adaptive to change, but driven by the fear of change itself, and its accompanying loss of 'naturalised' privileges. It seems to me that a progressive reading of the nation is unable to accommodate such regressive strategies, but must reject them as redundant. With the enclosure of the nationalist space at the turn of the century in the Western nation-state (and elsewhere) it is difficult to see them as redundant, albeit easy to recognise their regressive state.[19]

One fairly recent example of how the nationalist representation appears on the surface to be a call for national unity, but is in fact a deeply divisive device, was the national commemoration of the deceased cricket legend, Don Bradley, described by Prime Minister Howard as the greatest living Australian. Although national in scope this media-driven commemoration soon emerged as a problematic occasion for bringing together the nation, for although Bradley in his days as a cricketer may have represented a national sport, it is a sport, which has ceased to be the national sport, it was in his monocultural heyday. However, this is precisely where the meaning of Bradman's iconic status becomes interesting in its contemporary context. He represents a time, which Australians today *see* as monoculturally white, and largely British in its cultural make-up. Hence the 1950s are projected as a time when all Australians shared the same aspirations, the same cultural values, a time where representation operated

---

19. The use of the term 'enclosure' is a deliberate reference to Locke's concept of private property as an inalienable right for the individual. The nation's enclosure similarly represents an urgency to close off and squeeze out alternative visions of the nation, which may threaten the established order. This reading owes much to Gramsci's idea about the interplay between hegemony and consent, and Edward Said's reading of Gramsci. See Edward Said, *Orientalism* (Harmondsworth: Penguin, 1995), pp. 6-7.

inside a closed operational circuit with experience, a time when Australia was white because it regarded itself as white. In this enclosed system of self-representation it matters little that there were Aborigines and continental Europeans, or the few Asians who managed to bypass the strictly enforced racist immigration policy. They had no role to play then in relation to the espousal of a national identity, for the preferred policy was decisively assimilationist. This assimilationist moment in Australian history is reenacted in the massively covered media event that surrounded the death of Bradman, for contemporary continental Europeans, Asians and Aborigines have no role today to play in the contemporary celebration of Bradman's achievement, other than passive endorsement.[20] As such the staging of the 'Bradman event'[21] is aimed at singling out a monocultural celebration/ commemoration that can be acknowledged but never shaped by those outside Anglo-Irish derived Australian culture. These patterns of representations have continued their domination within a nationalist ideology much longer than the fact of an altered multicultural Australia should have allowed them to, if indeed representation was merely a reflection of 'the

20. Bradman represents only one of the most recent examples of a far more general representational pattern of white Anglo-Celtic heroes. Graeme Turner describes the general pattern in *Making it National*:

> The construction of the Australian national character underwriting 1980s nationalism was, of course, anything but new. The Australian it celebrated...was most often very familiar: the cheeky, resourceful larrikin who populates Henry Lawson's stories and who was enshrined as the 'national type' in the work of Russel Ward. This version of the national character is prescriptive, unitary, masculinist and excluding. It is not a version of national identity that reflects the diversity of ethnicities, cultural traditions and political interests that currently exist in this postcolonial nation-state... (p. 5).

21. I use the term 'Bradman event' to emphasise that this was a deliberate strategy encouraged not least by the Prime Minister, and one might even argue contrary to the wishes of the Bradman family, who argued in vain that Bradman deliberately avoided publicity. Of course, for the promoters of the Bradman event this only proved the modesty of the man....

Australian experience'.[22] Yet challenges are mounted from various quarters against the dominance of the white male national ethos. Hence Turner has argued how this representational pattern has come under siege from a number of, significantly, interdisciplinary discussions of Australian identity:

> Increasingly...the orthodoxies of Australian identity associated with 'the Australian legend' have become the subject of critiques which view them as mythic inventions carrying regressive consequences for the nation that believes in them...the disparities between the licensed batteries of national imagery and the 'realities' of national cultural experience is exposed as the consequence of longstanding discrimination, oppression and imperialism... the need has become pressing to reconsider the dominant, essentially nineteenth century, images commonly employed to represent Australian identity.[23]

Some of the most challenging criticism has come from feminism, and Turner singles out Margarey, Rowley and Sheridan's attack on Australian nationalism's idealisation of a masculine value system:

> For it is masculinity that is celebrated in assertions of an Australian culture that is independent of ties to any skirts — whether those ruling the domestic hearth, or those preaching from church pulpits, or those of the mother country — an Australian culture expressed in the virility of young men assaulting the virgin bush, remote from the corrupting centres of imperial rule, drawing emotional warmth and support from a homosocial camaraderie that has undertones of misogynist and racist violence not far below the surface.[24]

---

22. Turner makes a similar point on a more general level when he quotes Phillip Schlesinger who argues that:

> National cultures are not simple repositories of shared symbols to which the entire population stands in identical relation. Rather, they are to be approached as sites of contestation in which competition over definitions takes place. (*Making It National*, p. 10)

23. *Making It National*, p. 5.
24. Margarey, Rowley and Sheridan quoted in *Making It National*, p. 6.

The quotation is important because it demonstrates how Australian radical nationalism, e.g. in the shape of Russell Ward's famous assertion about the 'typical Australian', through its counter-position against a more openly British-derived conservative nationalism, has been invested with an innocence (and radicalism) that betrays its own imperialist origins. The exposure of that which is ignored by nationalist representation should not, however, lead one to the tempting conclusion that nationalist representations are largely static and redundant and hence easily dismissed and replaced with more dynamic readings of the nation's space. Turner points out the importance of recognising:

> The history of the 'uses' of nationalism in Australia over the last decade highlights, not these discourses' monolithic predictability, but their canny flexibility, their readiness for continual appropriation and deployment as they participate in the construction of a national culture.[25]

In order to challenge the nationalist discourse it is necessary to mount a critique that moves the focus away from the nationalist representational tropes, and instead expose the discursive foundations on which nationalist representations stand. To begin such a process I find it enabling to make use of the trope of representation, such as it has been employed by Edward Said in his seminal study *Orientalism*. However, I not only wish to discuss Said's understanding of representation as a general strategy to achieve and maintain hegemonic control, where nationalism may be seen as a particular instance of this desire to exert control of acceptable modes of national representation. I also wish to bring Said's understanding of orientalism as a discursive strategy to bear on my reading of Australian nationalism, and I will show how 'Asia' has operated in Australian nationalism, simultaneously as Australia's internalised and externalised 'other'. As such 'Asia' operates as a manifestation of an Australian orientalism. As Said points out orientalism operates as an internal discursive practice, which recycles particular assumptions about the 'Orient' and the 'Oriental' for internal consumption. However, just as Said

25. *Making It National*, p. 10.

distinguishes between English, French and American forms of orientalism, there is also a culturally situated orientalism at work in Australia. My understanding of how orientalism operates as the dominant way of conceptualising Australia's relationship with 'Asia', shares similarities with other people's work. Hence Nicholas Brown has pointed out how an Australian variant of orientalism has operated historically in Australia:

> White settlers in Australia have contributed their own distinctive emphases to the generic opposition between Asia as the East or the Orient, and European society as Western or Occidental. In the nineteenth century their image registered opportunities and anxieties perhaps more pressing than those informing the English convention of the Orient. A colonial rather than a metropolitan construction this image drew on influences ranging from the early schemes of entrepreneurs to fears of contamination and invasion. And, as Edward Said has argued of the European context, the Australian image was inherently reflexive — although what it reflected of colonial society was not so much the sophisticated patterns of an Orientalist discourse, operating across diverse fields from literature to strategy, but a more basic attempt to define the culture and the institutions of a new society in what was seen as an alien hemisphere.[26]

Brown's observation is perceptive, but framed within a specific historical context of Federation Australia. It is necessary to point out that such patterns of representation have not only grown out of a colonial and early national predicament that is resolved as Australians 'belatedly' embrace their hemisphere. The white anxieties have governed both attitudes to immigration (internalised) and international relations (externalised) with 'Asia', and in the current climate it is difficult to see that these attitudes have fundamentally changed.[27]

---

26. Nicholas Brown, 'Australian Intellectuals and the Image of Asia: 1920 1960' in *Australian Perceptions of Asia*. Special Issue of Australian Cultural History, no. 9, 1990 ed. by David Walker, Julian Horne and Adrian Vickers.
27. Ien Ang makes a similar point when she points out how xenophobia in Australia continues to labour under the weight of Australia's proximity to Asia and distance from Europe (*Alter/Asians*, p. xvii).

Ian Wedde makes the point succinctly when he describes Australia's image of its Asian other as governed by 'an "Asia" constructed not by its own "Asian" histories, but by a European history and cartography which has, up to this moment, viewed the Java seas between Asia and Australia as a quarantine moat rather than a cultural conduit'.[28]

Kuan-Hsing Chen makes a similar point, when he speaks of the consequences for the internalised Asian other in his discussion of the limits of a multicultural practice, through the example of Australia. Although Chen asserts that multiculturalism has replaced a far more oppressive assimilation policy and attitude, he also draws attention to the work of Ghassan Hage, who has pointed out that the fact:

> that multicultural policy 'allows' others to 'maintain their cultures' does not mean that it is 'not a fantasy of total control'.... 'Multicultural language in this regard is merely moving along with the language of zoology'...; like zoology, the system of multicultural language classifies others, constructs hierarchical orders, and as if in the zoo, minorities are displayed as rare animals. 'All ethnic cultures within the Anglo-Celtic multicultural collection are imagined as dead cultures that cannot have a life of their own except through the "peaceful co-existence" that regulates the collection'.[29]

But if Chen speaks of an internal 'othering' process where Wedde and Brown speak of a periodically located anxiety of an externalised Asian other, the conclusions they reach on the operation of this mechanism are remarkable similar. Hence Chen concludes:

> To reformulate Hage's theoretical articulation at a general level: if the cultural basis of colonialism is racism, and its cultural strategy, assimilation, which generates an identification with the aggressor/colonizer, then one can say that the cultural basis of neocolonialism is

28. Ian Wedde quoted in Pamela Hansford, 'The "Impossible" Aesthetic: Asia and Australian Visual Arts', in *Australia and Asia: Cultural Transactions*, ed. by Maryanne Dever (London: Curzon Press, 1997), p. 10.
29. *Trajectories: Inter-Asia Cultural Studies*, ed. by Kuan-Hsing Chen (London: Routledge, 1998), p. 21.

> multiculturalism (which recognizes differences but covers its dominant ethnic position as the nodal point of divide), and its cultural strategy, peaceful co-existence, and which generates an identification with the self in the form of nativism, civilizationalism and identity politics. The direction of an incomplete project of decolonization is then to interiorize others in a highly self-conscious manner; here 'others' are not simply racial, ethnic and national categories, but also class, sex/gender and geographical positionings.[30]

If Chen agrees with Brown as to the mechanisms of exclusion, it is difficult to see how they can agree about its transitional status versus a more permanent state. This is, of course, where their own positioning becomes relevant. Brown's stressing of a transitional phase of hostility followed by a more forthcoming attitude as the Australians gradually 'come to terms' with their new, alien environment, is an argument for a nation coming into being, a successful transplanting of one European civilisation into another Australian one. Chen denies this easy reconciliation between nature/Aborigine/other and European/white/self through an evolutionary adjustment. The implicit argument is that the binary opposition is intrinsic to the settlement process itself. The two positions are really an argument about the nature of modernity in its displaced settlement form in Australia.

Yet if Chen's reading tends to promote a pessimistic reading of the possibility of change, some discursive terrain has been opened, even on a general level. Hence David Day's history of Australia, *Claiming a Continent*, shows how Asia has operated as Australia's discursive other just as it has operated and continues to operate at a physical level as an other. This is, if not ground-breaking, then certainly path-breaking because it puts physically (and psychologically) to the forefront that which previous histories of Australia have not only downplayed, but at times even deliberately ignored. As such it displaces an earlier strategy which may be illustrated by the following example: When Manning Clark speaks of the instalment of a British civilisation in the Australian wilderness, this wilderness

30. *Trajectories*, p. 21.

exists both as nature, as a euphemism for Aboriginal failure to 'develop' a civilisation and as an implicit recognition of Australia as an isolated continent, not a continent on the outskirts of Asia, and a continent with a pre-settlement contact history with Asian (and other European) cultures, and as a continent that has seen a traffic of Aborigines arriving from Asia over enormous lengths of time.[31] What historians writing about the Australian nation have carried out is not only a chronological narration of the nation's past, it is a narration that is conditioned by selective criteria and visions that are in vogue in their own time of writing. As such it does also become the historian's projection of his own contemporaneity onto the past. Yet this is seldom foregrounded.

The departure I wish to take in this study is precisely to overtly focus on Australia's contemporary reorientation towards Asia, and trace back Australia's preoccupations with Asia through the Australian nation's representation of itself. It is my contention that although interest in Australia's relations with Asia have also awoken historically, for example in David Walker's book, *Anxious Nation,* it continues to be seen as separate from any process that has to do with the construction of a national identity.

More specifically I will take departure in the much-abused term 'Asian turn' that has taken place in Australian political discourse since the 1980s and which has become increasingly central to 'Australian studies'. Two ways of discussing the Asian turn in cultural studies present themselves immediately. First, one could ask how the Asian turn influences 'mainstream'

---

31. It is possible then to argue that Clark's and other historians' emphasis on the umbilical cord to Great Britain and European 'civilisation history' betrays an anxiety. It is a narrativisation of history that is haunted by another narrative of colonial oppression:

> The legacy of the colonial past is a continuing fear of illegitimacy, and an inability to develop the kind of pluralist inclusive account of the past that might form the basis for a coherent national community. Reconciliation, fervently desired in some quarters and despised and rejected in others, consequently remains unachievable in a society profoundly unsettled by *ressentiment,* and desperately seeking to hold onto foundational myths and sentiment which find little support elsewhere. (*The Australian Legend and Its Discontents,* p. 37)

books on Australian cultural history, and secondly, how a new critique has emerged from within Australian cultural studies from an 'Asian perspective'.

If we begin by looking at the international implications of an 'Asian approach', Wayne Hudson and Geoffrey Bolton's introduction to *Creating Australia* offers the following conceptualisation of what, to use Benedict Anderson's terminology may be called a 'comparative spectre'[32] between Australia and its 'Asian neighbours':

> During the last half century Australia has renegotiated its international relationships. No longer merely a far-flung outpost of the British Empire, nor a spectator of the competition for supremacy in the Western Pacific between the United States and Japan, today Australia is entering upon new relationships with the rest of the world, and notably with the nations of Southeast and East Asia. Malaysia and Indonesia, to say nothing of China, sometimes proclaim concepts of nationalism which strike a little harshly on Australian ears. We are accustomed to accepting criticism from overseas, the most pointed coming often from our traditional partners, the British and the Americans. For the tigers of Southeast Asia, however, criticisms from foreigners may be deemed an impertinence. We are habituated to abusing our politicians roundly and to examining their conduct searchingly. The political leaders of Southeast Asia are less receptive to challenge. Since our strategic and commercial future is intertwined with the new nationalism of Southeast Asia, it behoves us not only to cultivate a sensitive understanding of our neighbours' national self-concepts, but also to foster a more confident awareness of our own.[33]

32. There is a double-edge to my use of Anderson's term here. For on the one level it refers simply to the need to be aware of what uses a comparison serves, but also as Anderson points out in relation to his own experience in Indonesia, how he saw 'my Europe as through an inverted telescope', *The Spectre of Comparisons*, p. 2.
33. Wayne Hudson and Geoffrey Bolton, 'Creating Australia' in *Creating Australia*, p. 2.

Bolton and Hudson's entry is strategic to say the least, bordering on a smug self-congratulatory attitude to Australia's traditions. Corruption is seen as endemic to Southeast Asia, whereas in Australia the revelation of corruption is seen as proof of the system's soundness. The Howard government's dismissal of international criticism in the wake of the Tampa affair and detention centre scandals would seem to call at least for some measure of adjusting the absolute nature of such an assertion.[34]

However, what I find more interesting in the present context is how Bolton and Hudson tackle the 'Asian turn'. It is at first a paradoxical feature of their approach that although speaking of a new departure for Australia's relations with 'Asia', it is the limited scope of such a new relationship which defines their approach. Indeed it is tempting to use the term 'damage control' about the eagerness with which they speak only of 'strategic and commercial future', rather than an active engagement, or cultural exchange that has already been happening for some time when Hudson and Bolton wrote their introduction. What also emerges is the idea of a nation already formed, not only in terms of territoriality but also in terms of attitudes. Hudson and Bolton's position is conditioned by a highly strategic reading of Australian settlement history, which does not mention the White Australia policy, although that is the cornerstone of the overwhelmingly non-Asian settlement history. Nor does it mention the White Australia policy's opposite, that is, the long, albeit disrupted, and curbed immigration from Asia. But even more important in the contemporary context no mention is made of the significant level of Asian immigration since the collapse of the White Australia policy, and what such an influx might mean to

34. The poor critical standards offered by mainstream Australian media and the public support for Howard's refugee policy speak volumes about the anxieties which continue to inform the vast majority of Australians' attitudes towards 'Asia', even if throughout Australian history the overt target has changed from China to Japan, to Vietnam, to Indonesia and, most recently, to Iraq, Afghanistan and the Middle East. The shape of the target has also gone through different stages although it has usually fluctuated between physical invasion fears, and the fear of 'aliens seeping in'.

definitions of Australian identity, and to ways of dealing with the homelands of these migrants. Instead what is asserted here, is that criticism of Australia comes from its friends (*i.e.* sameness), while what is deemed as characteristic of 'Asia' is difference. In quite stereotypical fashion Hudson and Bolton assert a set of implicitly positive Australian characteristics against a set of predictable, negative Asian characteristics. The reservations about the nature of Australia's engagement with Asia which Hudson and Bolton's view betrays are explored in Maryanne Dever's introduction to *Australia and Asia: Cultural Transactions* (London: Curzon Press, 1997), where she comments:

> as Chua Siew Keng has observed, the 'push into Asia' can be read on one level as a strategic redeployment of a traditional 'us' and 'them' dichotomy, serving to keep 'Asians' in 'Asia' and Australia 'emphatically white'.... The sanctioned goal of 'enmeshment', it would appear, is 'Australia in Asia', a potentially neo-colonialist strategy of national aggrandisement, and not 'Asia in Australia', the marker instead of a potentially threatening boundary instability. Journalist Lachlan Colquhoun made this precise point when...he observed that 'the boat people show Australians — more than any number of trade deals or air links — that they are part of Asia, but expose their unpreparedness for Asia to be part of Australia'.[35]

Asia disappears from any narrative of the Australian nation more or less as soon as it has served its purpose within the limits defined by a nationalist rhetoric of self-definiton. The paradoxes imbedded in such a cultural definition of self have been brilliantly exposed by the Chinese-Australian poet, Ouyang Yu, in his poem: Australia is not Asia/ has not to like Australia (and so forth), which confirms the umbilical cord that ties together the Australian self with its Asian other.[36] At one level this curious and paradoxical Australian attitude may then be seen as a manifestation of the other emerging through the

---

35. *Australia and Asia: Cultural Transactions*, ed. by Maryanne Dever (London: Curzon Press, 1997), p. 3.
36. I discuss Ouyang Yu's poetry further in a later chapter.

cracks of nationalist discourse. It may also be seen as a shallowness of engagement that has followed in the wake of the much discussed Asian turn, which amounts to little more than a grudging acknowledgement of the Asian nations' existence and geographical proximity, or the anxiety driven narrative of their circumscribed impact on Australia. The differences upheld as a mirror of distortion between Australia and its Asian neighbours serve to assert Australia's Western identity. By this I do not mean that Australia really is an Asian (or an Aboriginal) nation, but that the process of legitimating an illegitimate colonial invasion continues to haunt the Australian nation's range of self-perceptions, externally *vis-à-vis* Asia and internally *vis-à-vis* Asian migrants and the indigenous peoples. The need to justify Australia as a Western nation, awkwardly placed at the wrong end of the world, leads to the need to justify Australia position ironically through a displacement of its geo-political location. Australia is a Western civilisation *because* it is not an Asian country with a predisposition to despotic rulers and rapidly growing, volatile populations. This in spite of the fact that Australia has participated in more wars than its Asian neighbours through its short history as a nation-state, and is at least partly responsible for wars in Asia on two occasions.[37]

To uphold the mirror of difference between Australia and Asia it is necessary also to regard the countries inside this comparative spectre as given entities. The comparison of competitive nations (even cultures and civilisations) operate simultaneously as a spatial division of difference, a cultural divide between on the one side an Australian (Western) liberal democracy, utopian and idealistic in its aspirations; and on

37. It is now an established fact that it was an important part of Australian foreign policy to secure American military presence on the Asian mainland, and that Australian governments actively encouraged Americans to intervene in Indochina. It is also an established fact that Australia condoned the Indonesian invasion of Portuguese Timor. The Whitlam and subsequently the Fraser government may not have foreseen the scale of the carnage which followed. However, neither did they protest, but stood out in their eager recognition of the Indonesian invasion as a *de facto* incorporation of Portuguese Timor as an Indonesian province.

the other side an Australian Oriental other; characterised by despotism, dystopia and the abuse of human rights. Both sets of characteristics are seen to be generated by internal forces. Colonalism and neo-colonialism, Western complicitness in the often internal rather than external abuses perpetrated by marionets put there by the West to safeguard the (economic) interests of the 'international community' is simply absent from such accounts.

This is how the division is seen now, but obviously it is but the latest manifestation of a pattern of responses to Asia which can be traced throughout Australia's European settlement history. The anxiety to identify Australia squarely with perceived Western ideals — of dressing Australia up in the garb of 'western civilisation' — is not particularly Australian, but typical of western attitudes. However, the Australian case becomes interesting, because of an added edge in the Australian context, for the regional Australian patent on perceived Western ideals operates simultaneously through a temporal and geographical displacement. The temporal displacement operates through Australia's double position as colonised and colonising, whereas the geographic displacement operates through immediacy. The rejection of alternatives to Australia's embrace of Western modernity is arguably more urgent, because its dealings with the non-Western are not negotiated through the safe distancing offered by certain protective measures available to Europe and the US, neither in economic nor in relative geographical terms.[38]

If we turn from the 'external Asia' to consider the response from the 'internalised Asia' to the 'Asian turn', what departures do they offer for a reconsideration of Australian cultural history from a far more inclusive historical/political/cultural practice?

Certainly an 'Asian turn' has taken place in Australian studies. This fact is clear from numerous new titles, which have emerged over the last 5-10 years. This plethora of studies can be seen as an extension or expansion of the multicultural

---

[38] Ironically, the waves of refugees from Asia which Australia cannot control through an immigration policy alone, have not come from the nearest populous nation, Indonesia, but via Indonesia from Western Asia and China.

debate within Australian studies, yet it may also be discussed in terms of these studies' ability to open a new practice which will displace existing models of Australian culture. Two books, *Alter/Asians*[39] and *Diaspora: Negotiating Asian-Australia*[40] invite particular attention here, because they specifically place the 'Asian turn' in Australian culture (here defined in the broadest of its meanings), at the centre of their focus. As Ien Ang points out in her introduction to *Alter/Asians*, after having stated the economic and political reorientation of Australia towards Asia: 'What are the cultural implications if this shift? And how does the idea of "Australia in Asia" relate to the increasing visibility of "Asians in Australia"?'[41]

The distinction Ang makes between an internalised and an externalised perspective on what on the surface level appears as a functionalistic question, quickly emerges as a problem about patterns of representation:

> Intellectual engagement with Asia/Australia relationships is intense, but its articulation remains ambivalent and still biased towards a sense of panic or alarm. Despite the rhetoric of tolerance, the presence of Asians within Australia continues to be seen as a problem for social cohesion, and Australia's regional engagement with Asia is seen either as a political liability or a mere conduit for economic prosperity (via trade, tourism or educational export).[42]

The (xenophobic, racist or at least deeply ambivalent sets of) representations which govern nationalist Australian responses to the Asian inside and the Asia outside are in Ang's view countered by a reality of change through the increased Asian demographic component 'in art and everyday life, in media and popular culture'.[43] To Ang they constitute an irreversible

39. *Alter/Asians: Asian-Australian identities in art, media and popular culture*, ed. by Ien Ang, Sharon Chalmers, Lisa Law and Mandy Thomas (Sydney: Pluto Press, 2000).

40. *Diaspora: Negotiating Asian-Australia*, ed. by Helen Gilbert, Tseen Khoo and Jacqueline Lo, a special issue of *Journal of Australian Studies*, no. 65, and *Australian Cultural History*, no. 19, 2000.

41. *Alter/Asians*, p. xiii.

42. *Alter/Asians*, p. xiv.

43. *Alter/Asians*, p. xv.

process, but as long as the 'inside' remains unconnected with the 'outside', it is difficult to see how they necessarily constitute a change, other than in both cases a grudging acknowledgement of their presence. If the two were connected it would on the other hand signal unequivocally a new departure for what is defined as Australia's interests across the board, as well as lead to an active engagement with the Asian within and Asia without. Without such an active involvement the manufacturing of 'an Asian turn' need not in itself challenge let alone lead to a change in the nationalist definitions of what constitutes an Australian experience. Australian history provides us already with one example of this: The much more established continental European migrants have, although they have provided much of the platform for establishing a multicultural practice, not managed to dislodge the nationalist iconography of the Anglo-Irish majority. It is perhaps with this awareness of the difference between manifest experience and representations that Ang makes the following dismal observation:

> Yet there has hardly been any serious intellectual reflection so far on these cultural developments, their complex social and political implications, and the multiple contestations and contradictions necessarily attending them.... Most importantly, there is still hardly any public recognition in Australia of Asian Australians as subjects of representation, as intellectuals, artists or writers vigorously intervening in, and making inroads into the dominant culture, and as active makers of culture in their own right.... There is even less recognition of the complex set of transnational relations and cross-cultural social formations of Asian Australians, connections that may be social, economic and which may span several continents and dramatically impact upon everyday experiences of Asians living in Australia and, in turn, on Australian culture more generally.
>
> This book aims to open up the emergent cultural space of Asian Australia through a decisive shift away from the all-too-familiar treatment of 'Asians' as other.[44]

44. *Alter/Asians*, p. xv.

The concluding remark as to what the collection of essays is meant to achieve sits rather oddly with the more dismal view of the record so far. Furthermore, unless it accepts this 'emergent cultural space' as an enclosure within a largely unchanged nationalist space for representations that continues to construct images of Asia/ns as other, it surely needs to challenge those representational standards. Otherwise the most it can hope for, as far as changing the boundaries of Australian representations is concerned, is merely to repeat the previous experience with other now demographically 'established' migrant groups. 'Established' because as I have pointed out tolerance of presence needs not in itself lead to a change in the nation's self-representation. Instead it can easily be read as a strategy of containment, precisely because the majority culture cannot afford to totally ignore the 'Asian component' as it could not in the long term afford to ignore the presence of the post-war wave of European migrants. Hence a very modestly challenging presence in the polity of the nation was allowed through the trope of multiculturalism. I am not making this point to dismiss the possibility of change, but to question the progressionist narrative of the nation, which seems to govern Ang's reading of the migrant situation in Australia. Behind her progressionist narrative lies an anxiety that substantially nothing has changed, a fear that emerges from her own ambivalent remarks later in the introduction:

> The predominant definition of Asianness in Australia still depends on the lumping together of all of 'Asia' as if it were a monolithic entity, on a process of racial/cultural othering that still continues to be reproduced, for example, in media representations of 'Asia' or even in some well-intentioned efforts to bring 'Asian' art to the Australian public. Paradoxically, however, one might speculate that it is precisely the perceived absolute difference — the felt incommensurability — of all people and things 'Asian' that has impelled the sense of urgency with which the relationship between 'Asia' and 'Australia' has been addressed in the closing years of the twentieth century.[45]

45. *Alter/Asians*, p. xviii.

The problem with Ang's position is that she is caught between, on the one hand, the thought that modernity represents the solution to the gradual break-up of a traditional Australian monopoly on nationalist representations, while, on the other hand, she sees the Australian nation model as contingent upon 'Asian othering'. The first point suggests an evolutionary adjustment of the nation, while the second point requires a radical transformation.[46] The irreconcilable juxtaposition of two incommensurable approaches to understanding ways in which to bring about change in the nation's selfhood, leads Ang to conclude on a note which may be correct in its identification of strategies for understanding the processes of cultural change in Australia, but which is in important ways also contradictory:

> As a result it is the *interface* between 'Asia' and 'Australia' that has become the site of cultural negotiation and contestation — a process in which an increasing number of Asian Australians take an active part.[47]

Hope here appears to be pinned on role models who will pave the way for future generations of Asians, in spite of Ang's own reservations about the nature of the change brought

---

46. I am not alone with these reservations. Hence I find Ang's attempt to posit two antagonistic strategies problematic also in the light of Suvendrini's observation in the same collection on the operations of a white nationalist discourse in Australia:

    > The white nativist discourse of Hansonism temporalises and spatialises the narratives of Australia's history through a range of moves: it erases the time prior to colonisation, casting it as unproductive, empty and meaningless time, and so legitimising its own claim to the land; second, it consolidates this claim to ownership by casting 'the Asian' as the alien and invader figure, thus (re)usurping the place of the indigene; and, finally, it constructs a script of assimilation in which selected groups of other successive migrants are progressively racialised as 'white'. (*Alter/Asians*, p. 17)

    It is difficult not to see Hansonism as an extreme, but also as merely a particularly brutal form of a much wider Anglo-Irish dominated discourse on nationalist representation of Australian selfhood. How this is to be reconciled with a more evolutionary conceptualisation of change in nationalist representation is difficult to grasp.
47. *Alter/Asians*, p. xviii.

on by multiculturalism for older established continental European migrants.

In the opening essay of *Alter/Asians*, 'Futures Imperfect', Suvendrini Perera takes a far more sceptical attitude to the politics of change in Australian culture. Perera establishes a more radicalised reading position from which it becomes possible to begin to posit alternative versions of Australian cultural history. Perera calls for:

> histories and forms of cultural relations that are outside dominant theorisations of Australian history, whether it is presented as a drama of binary black/white relations, or, as is often the case where questions of multiculturalism are acknowledged, as an unequal triangle in which 'migrants', and especially 'Asians', form a kind of belated third, or supplement, to the central conflict of black vs white. These are the two major models we currently have for writing about Australian cultural relations — what I'll call the binary model and the supplement model. Indeed, one might say that indigenous peoples and non-Anglo migrants rarely meet in the space or time of Australian history books, because Aborigines usually occupy the first chapter, and 'migrants' the last chapter.[48]

If, as Perera argues, the existing models for conceptualising the Australian nation are redundant, the question arises how one might begin to contemplate alternative histories, which not only expand what falls inside Australian culture, but also challenge received histories aimed at consolidating the Anglo-Irish hold on the nation's selfhood. Perera provides two examples, which begin to address creatively what my study seeks to do in a more literal sense. The second example[49] is Bruce Pascoe's novel *Ruby-Eyed Coucal*, which, argues Perera:

> imagines the possibility of mounting a legal challenge to the principle of *terra nullius* based on ancient trade

48. *Alter/Asians*, pp. 11-12.

49. Significantly, Perera's other example engages in a similar challenge of the predominant form of nationalist representation of the nation's others.

> and cultural links between China, Indonesia, Papua New Guinea and the peoples of Arnhem Land. This is a contact that long predates the arrival of Captain Cook.... By writing a counter-history of international and regional relations prior to the imposition of *terra nullius*, Pascoe challenges the very concept of Australia as an isolated and singular entity cut off from 'civilisation' until it was 'discovered' in 1770. Instead, he posits a pre-existing mesh of complex and sophisticated kinship, cultural and trade exchanges between the places we now know as Irian Jaya, Papua New Guinea and the northern coast of Arnhem Land. The new geocultural configuration represented here counters any notion of Australia as fundamentally separate from Asia.[50]

Perera's example identifies precisely the point of departure for my own study, particularly through the foregrounding of Pascoe's juxtaposition of Aborigines and Asians. As Perera points out the novel 'reconfigures the space of Australia, not as an island entire unto itself, but as made up of different cultural and national spaces which share histories and borders with other regional peoples and societies'.[51] In terms of nationalist representations in contemporary Australia this alternative history of Australian cultural history goes a long way to explain the othering of Asians and Aborigines. For it is premised on these groups' potential ability to challenge the very foundation on which Anglo-Irish/Australian definitions of nationhood rest, and as such they cannot be included through expansionist Australian cultural historical representations. Their inclusion requires a rewriting that foregrounds the racial history, which ironically is there for all to see in Australian history, but not often there to be written about, except for in dismissive terms as far as wider national implications are concerned.

The Four Chapters

In the following four Chapters I wish to lay bare, challenge and open up the discursive practices which inform dominant

50. *Alter/Asians*, p. 16.

51. *Alter/Asians*, p. 16.

patterns of representations, by dealing with four quite different aspects of Australian cultural history which are nonetheless bound together by the same limitations.

The first chapter explores the historical discourse on Australia's colonial beginnings. It shows that such representations of historical beginnings are important as their own contemporaneity's imagining and construction of Australia's colonial beginnings. Here it is possible to speak in temporal as well as spatial terms of Australia's beginnings. Hence the singular focus on the well-recorded beginning at Sydney Cove has tended to overshadow both what happened elsewhere and what happened prior to this settlement. Australia has many colonial beginnings, some of which lie outside the British-Australian domain. However, through a singular focus on one event as *the* beginning, the national history has become unitary, untamperable with and taken for granted. Subsequent historiographical discourse has as a consequence ended up focusing on two (equally nationalistic) interpretations of that history; either as the instalment of a hierarchically formed British civilisation and its subsequent Australian derivation, or as the insertion of a radically (trans)formed new identity as anti-authoritarian, republican and horizontal, defined as a break, or a series of breaks, with a British tradition. Both interpretations rest, however, within a largely male Anglo-Irish defined universe, which leaves little room for the consideration of other cultural histories as meaningful contributions to an Australian identity.

Chapter 2 begins to map out an alternative way of representing Australian history, through the optic of Asia, by discussing Aboriginal relations with Asia, prior to and during the colonial phase in North Australia. The purpose of this Chapter is threefold. First, I wish to challenge the current, preferred mode of representing Aborigines as largely isolated people, an image which feeds into a long established view of Aboriginal culture as static. I wish to counter that dominant representation by showing how patterns of dynamic cultural exchange had evolved between Aborigines in Northern Australia and their Asian 'neighbours'. This exchange was in fact stopped through the incursion by the newly independent Australian federation into its border zones. As such this history shows the emerging nation-state seeking to justify its own presence through an aggressive assertion of territorial control, particularly at those border zones whose existence most evidently betrays both the nation's constructedness and its horizontal expansion as a centralised, imposing power.

Secondly, the predominantly static view of Aboriginal culture is also a precondition for accepting the 'fact and act' of the white invasion in 1788. Halting Aboriginal-Asian cultural exchanges may have been primarily due to economic considerations, and defence anxieties, but it also conveniently helped to confirm the view of an isolated and static Aboriginal society, unable to cope with the dynamics of change. When the Aborigines refused to die out, succeeding governments sought to 'whiten' them out of existence. That this operates on a popular level is clear from the support granted to the silencing of the assimilationist (some say genocidal) practices of Australian governments for decades in the twentieth century, but it survives equally well in much academic discourse in Australia. It is still possible to write on Australian cultural history and either bypassing this process or seeing it as an unfortunate by-product of an otherwise benevolent society, a fact that shows that discourse is less a question about knowledge than it is about ideological platforms, the production of knowledge, and the legitimisation of viewpoints. Both this Chapter and Chapter 1 uses a historiographical approach to discuss how the nation represents itself through particular discourses, but also how alternative visions are waiting for those who wish to employ them.

Chapter 3 continues the problematisation of the nation's representation of self, this time through the externalised Asian other. In this Chapter I discuss Australia's engagement with its arguably principal Asian other, Indonesia, and focus on the interrelations from the phase of Indonesian decolonisation to what has been described as the debacle of East Timor. I argue that there has momentarily been opportunities of a more independent and more locally anchored Australian politics, but unfortunately they have remained momentary as Australian governments have quickly sought the approval of 'powerful allies' at the expense of a more localised approach. The East Timor crisis could be read as one moment when

Australia had the window of opportunity to take upon itself a moral and ethical responsibility, but largely abandoned these principles in favour of its own economic and strategic interests.

Chapter 4 turns to the consideration of 'Asia in Australia' via a discussion of the long migration history of the Chinese as one significant manifestation of a multicultural history that casts its shadow over all of Australia's non-Aboriginal history. As such the Chapter represents an alternative cultural strand within the nation's narrative, which challenges the nation's preferred ways of representing itself and opens for more inclusive, more productive and cross-culturally based understandings of a national Australian space.

What is shared by these four Chapters that might otherwise be seen as separate interventions into constructions of national identity in Australia, is the challenging of a particularist reading of the nation's mental territory which has been established as *the* only generally acceptable reading of the nation. The elevation of a particularist settlement narrative to the level of a general history of Australia serves the purpose of exclusively defining what constitutes an Australian experience, to the detriment of other experiences. Also, it is necessary to elevate the plethora of multicultural narratives from their compartmentalised existence in order to make use of their potential as a powerful critique of the received model of national evolution. For evolutionary is the accurate term with which to describe both conservative and radical nationalist formulations about Australian identities. They rest on the assumption of a shared experience, even when that experience is indeed premised on deeply antagonistic positions within the representation as well as being preconditioned on the exclusion of other 'non-nationalist' experiences. This binary system, however, is a byproduct of all nationalistic experience and representation. In the case of Australia the usual suspects are easily drummed up: Convicts vs. Officers, Officers vs. Governors (or sometimes with), British vs. Aborigines, white Australians vs. Aborigines, golddiggers vs. colonial Establishment, 'Australian' golddiggers vs. Chinese golddiggers, and the split during the Boer War and World War I concerning conscription and participation in the war. Something which is totally written out of the allegiance paid to soldiers of the

First World War, who by the way might not even have wanted to be paid allegiance to, but might rather have preferred, as one of its participants, A.B. Facey, has pointed out, a commemoration of the futility of war and the waste of human life.

REFERENCES

Alter/Asians: Asian-Australian identities in art, media and popular culture, ed. by Ien Ang, Sharon Chalmers, Lisa Law and Mandy Thomas (Sydney: Pluto Press, 2000).

Anderson, Benedict, *Imagined Communities: Reflections on the Origin and Spread of Nationalism* (London: Verso, 1991).

Anderson, Benedict, *The Spectre of Comparisons: Nationalism, Southeast Asia, and the World* (London: Verso, 1998).

Ang, Ien and Jon Stratton, 'Asianing Australia: Notes toward a critical transnationalism in cultural studies', *Cultural Studies* (10) 1 1996: pp. 16-36.

Australia and Asia: Cultural Transactions, ed. by Maryanne Dever (London: Curzon Press, 1997).

Australian Cultural Studies: A Reader, ed. by John Frow and Meaghan Morris (Chicago: University of Illinois Press, 1993) *Australian Perceptions of Asia.* Special Issue of Australian Cultural History, no. 9, 1990 ed. by David Walker, Julian Horne and Adrian Vickers.

Creating Australia: Changing Australian History, ed. by Wayne Hudson and Geoffrey Bolton (Sydney: Allen & Unwin, 1997).

Day, David, *Claiming a Continent* (Sydney: Harper Collins, 2001).

Diaspora: Negotiating Asian-Australia, ed. by Helen Gilbert, Tseen Khoo and Jacqueline Lo, a special issue of *Journal of Australian Studies*, no. 65, and *Australian Cultural History*, no. 19, 2000.

Bruce Kapferer, *Legends of People, Myths of State* (London: Smithsonian Institute Press, 1998).

Morris, Meaghan, 'On the Beach', in Lawrence Grossberg, Cary Nelson and Paula Treichler (eds.) *Cultural Studies* (London: Longman, 1992), pp. 450-73.

Stratton, Jon and Ien Ang, 'On the Impossibility of a Global Cultural Studies: British Cultural Studies in an International Frame, in *Stuart Hall: Critical Dialogues in Cultural Studies*, ed. by David Morley and Kuan-Hsing Chen (London: Routledge, 1996), pp. 361-91.

The Australian Legend and Its Discontents, ed. by Richard Nile (St. Lucia, Qld: UQP, 2000).

Trajectories: Inter-Asia Cultural Studies, ed. by Kuan-Hsing Chen (London: Routledge, 1998).

Turner, Graeme, *Making It National: Nationalism and Australian Popular Culture* (Sydney: Allen & Unwin, 1994).

1

INFINITE REHEARSALS: HISTORIOGRAPHY AND AUSTRALIAN BEGINNINGS

> Historical events, like mountain ranges, can best be surveyed as a whole by an observer who is placed at a good distance from them. Out of the welter of acrimony, stratagem, ambition, generous impulses, lofty aspirations, meanness, selfishness, patriotism, and all the other motive forces amid which the work of the world gets itself done, emerge at length clear to the view certain shining personalities, certain determinations fluent in consequences, which are the stuff of which history is made.
>
> [Ernest Scott, *A Short History of Australia* (Melbourne: Oxford U.P., 1920), p. 308]

Australian cultural historians have devoted much time and energy to define and describe the evolution of a distinct Australian identity within the predominantly European transplanted culture. Particular sites in Australian historiography are picked upon, and quite often fought over, and watersheds that indicate a new, self-consciously Australian departure from a colonial mentality, away from an earlier more clearly defined British-Irish derived tradition, are presented. There are two schools that can be located within the debates concerning the nature of such new departures. One gives voice to a conservative view that emphasises a gradual and evolutionary transition from a largely unreflected identification with the British to an Australian outlook, but still ensconced in a framework of largely shared values. This school stresses the underlying continuity of British values and the shared cultural traditions of the Australians and the

British, downplaying the significance of more radical and oppositional elements, such as (particularly the Irish) convicts and 'migrants', who, in such conservative narratives, are marginalised as alienated elements outside Australian mainstream culture.

The other school represents a radical tradition that sees Australian culture as arising from a series of radical breaks from a British based, hierarchical value system, which is understood to be intrinsically alien to Australians. This school regards British and Australian values as essentially opposite, even antagonistic, particularly in accounts which portray the Irish strand in colonial history as crucial and central to the formation of an Australian identity. Battles between the two schools are fought over the interpretation of important events and experiences in Australian history. Popular themes include the nature of the early penal settlements, whether bushrangers embody Australian attitudes, the degree and importance of an egalitarian ethos among the golddiggers, the settlers as gentlemen of the bush or battlers against a hostile environment, and finally the Anzac legacy.

While the differences between these two schools have long been the subject of Australian academic discussions, I wish to alter the focus here and instead demonstrate how they both, in fact, converge, in crucial ways, and betray an assimilationist and exclusivist attitude. Hence it is my contention that both the conservative and radical nationalist school convey an unproblematised nationalist perspective through a critical stance determined by their mutual opposition. The problem lies less with the chosen strategies inside the battlefield, and far more with the demarcation of the battlefield itself. For in the process of taking issue with the antagonistic reading, they, in fact, reproduce the conditions under which the other reading becomes nationalist, and both fail as a consequence to take in more far-reaching critiques of what a nationalist perspective generally takes for granted. The point where the convergence between the two supposedly opposite readings is most clearly exposed, is in the construction of the Anzac myth. In both readings of the Anzacs (and particularly the landing of troops at Gallipoli) the blood sacrifice is presented as uncontestable evidence of the moment when

Australia gains its maturity as a nation. On the one hand, in the conservative reading, the Anzacs' supposed enunciation of Australian attitudes is regarded as the perfection of British values. The physical prowess of the Anzacs is seen as the proof that the Australian environment has perfected British character traits. The radical tradition, on the other hand, cites the same traits as evidence of the superiority of Australian egalitarian attitudes, emphasising their difference from hierarchical, tradition-bound British values. Such battles over the significance of the most important national myth cannot be reduced to a question of different readings of Gallipoli in its historical context. The battle between a hierarchical (conservative nationalist) and an egalitarian (radical nationalist) reading of Gallipoli has much more to do with the argument over what sort of place Australia is today. This argument manifests itself in displaced form in the nationalist celebration during the Anzac Day parades as either a commemoration of the shared Imperial history, or as a day which gives expression to Australian egalitarian values. The foregrounding of the disagreement over the meaning of Gallipoli clouds over the epistemological common ground of the two schools. Hence they both pave over the built-in paradoxes and contradictions between what is being commemorated and what controls the act of commemorating, as Alan Seymour's play, *The One Day of the Year*, reveals. The disparity between the play's performative controversy and its perceived controversial status is an apt illustration of the commemorative inconsistencies surrounding this day. Such inconsistencies derive from the split between the military campaign and individual and collective heroism on the one hand and, on the other hand, the need to recognise that the Australian soldiers were used (and let themselves be used) to further military-political imperial interests. The unity of the nation's determination to fight for the British is a post-war construction, and the endless recycling of war heroism serves to confirm the later construction of the national myth. Both nationalist schools have erected a myth surrounding the military prowess of the soldiers, dismissing any critique as suspect and equal to questioning the dedication and capability of the soldiers themselves. The conflation between the act of commemorating and the historical event itself is deliberate and covers up the lingering colonial cringe and white Australian anxiety, which generated the war hysteria that propelled and forced Australians into action in the first place. Furthermore, it cuts off the construction of the legacy from the wider context of the battle. This creates a narrow narrative strand that links the battle of Gallipoli with the legacy of nationalist heroics, dismissing questions such as how a battle taking place 15,000 km away can in any meaningful way be seen as a struggle for Australia's survival. It is, then, tempting and easy to see the contemporary marches, which for natural causes no longer involve veterans from World War I, as an act which aims to demonstrate the continued adherence to the dominant myth about Australia's birth as a nation. Inside the overall umbrella of blood sacrifice for the nation, conservative and radical readings can coexist through their separate, yet parallel, nationalistic, and hegemonic perspectives. As such Anzac Day becomes a manifestation of a selective, homogenising representation of the national self that overrides other more diverse representations. Although the selective inclusion of veterans from the Vietnam War, after years of non-recognition as heroic material, suggests that the commemoration is not static, its acts of inclusion are assimilationist. Although the participation of these veterans in the marches together with the political establishment who sent them to the vastly unpopular war could be seen as an act of national reconciliation, it is important to remember in what light their march should be seen. These marches operate inside a nationalist discourse that promotes the celebration of Australian democratic values, which in turn are tied in with a common imperial past in World War I, and with fighting against perceived Asian threats in the 1940s, 1950s and 1960s. Any involvement outside these 'campaigns' are regarded with suspicion as an unwelcome intrusion, and even threatening to a cohesive Australian value system. Interpretations over Australian identity may be at loggerheads over its egalitarian versus its British derived content, but they both pay allegiance to the white and male chronological order of mythical heroes culminating with the Anzacs, and carried on by the soldiers during World War II.

The aim with these introductory remarks is not to embark on a demolition of Australian myths, even if they do invite further exploration of the mechanisms producing such myths. Instead the comments demarcate a point of departure for exploring alternative ways of representing Australian identity formation that are less prone to accusations of exclusivist and assimilationist attitudes. Instead of identity models, which emphasise either monocultural traits or the possibility of extending this model to include Australia's multicultural diversity, I wish to examine Australian identity formation as it is represented in Australian historiography through the trope of 'difference'. I will focus on one particular period that is at the centre of Australian historiographic discourses, both to discuss the ways in which patterns of representation have evolved in Australian historiography, and to see how such patterns are related to debates on Australian identity in contemporary Australia. I have chosen to focus on the foundation of the first settlement at Sydney in 1788, and how that event has been rehearsed in later Australian historiography, both in history writing *per se*, but also within a broader nationalist context of representations.

The process of rehearsals reaches its climax in 1988 with the Australian Bicentennial, a year where commemoration fluctuated between historical re-enactment and a whole series of re-interpretations, which ranged from unconditional celebration to more critical interpretations, seizing upon the opportunity to raise issues that had been repressed by officially endorsed representations.

A Beginning

Australian historiography has been haunted by the mammoth work of Manning Clark. It has long been commonplace to find fault with his historical practice, and, what is more interesting in this context, the argument over his achievement has also shifted the focus on his achievement away from empirical reality and on to more historiographical considerations. It is important to draw attention to the discussions on Clark's achievement as a historian because the debate on Clark reveals the way in which his critics position themselves within Australian historiography, before going on to consider how different historical representational forms have operated in connection with the Australian Bicentennial.

The first collective effort to consider Clark's contribution to Australian historiography, *Manning Clark: Essays on His Place in History*, opens with a consideration of the many roles assigned to Clark as a historian, and points to the major contribution of this volume towards reaching a better understanding of Clark. Yet the focus is not unequivocally on Clark's achievement as a historian: 'Most important, questions are answered about his contribution to the debate about "Australian identity"'.[52] It is evident from the essays which follow this introduction that the evaluation of Clark depends heavily on the reading strategy applied. At one end of the spectre traditional historians devoted to the practice of conclusions drawn from detailed source material totally dismiss Clark's work. They are appalled by his sloppiness with facts. Behind their dismissal, however, lurks the uncomfortable awareness about the inconclusive exercise of representing historical events. At the other end of the spectre, commentators, who are more interested in his narrative departure from an older, empiricist tradition, praise his open, humanistic approach to his subject, some to the extent of ignoring his disregard of evidence. The responses from this camp are more interesting in a cultural historical context, and they demand a different approach from that of the traditional historians. Here, of course, Hayden White's *Metahistory* becomes an important general historiographical reference point, as well as the more overtly literary critical approaches in the volume, which are primarily concerned with how Clark narrates his history of Australia. To read Clark as a narrative historian seems to be the only relevant position to take, since the rejection of his incomplete and at times distorted representation of Australian history is too easy, and hence not particularly productive.[53] Even when taking his narrative

52. *Manning Clark: Essays on His Place in History,* ed. by Carl Bridge (Melbourne, Melbourne U.P., 1994), p. 2.

53. Manning Clark's representation of Australian history has been criticised from a number of sources, some of them in quite damning ways, including a criticism of his lack of historical accuracy. Also his outdated mode of history writing has been targeted, and his neglect of Aborigines,

form as a starting point there is a whole spectre of responses from those who discuss Clark's *History* in relation to the way it stages historical events, to those who simply relate to it as a chronological narrative of Australia. Hence one proposal by J.S. Ryan is to read Clark's *History* as an epic:

> The method [Clark] used is that of secondary/written or literary epic.... It differs from the individualistic ethic of primitive or oral epic in having a different conception of human worth and, despite looking to the past for inspiration, is inevitably being shaped by the present — a highly organised society where unfettered individualism should have no place.... Religious or otherwise, all secondary epic appeals to the desire for 'glory' or national respect and the duty to serve or even sacrifice oneself.[54]
>
> The parallels [from epic form] to the general content of Clark's *History* are clear: the long, serious national narrative; the 'subjective' exploration of 'origin' myths and of their continuing impact; the seedtime for the nation's ultimate fortunes; and a personal and even idiosyncratic treatment of received history.[55]

J.S. Ryan's account of Clark's contribution to understanding modern Australia is interesting, because it argues for the need to see Clark outside more conventional configurations of historical representation, but this raises two related points: Where is the epic coming from, and how is it possible to read Clark's History as epic without simultaneously rejecting its merits as history writing? Ryan's reading of Clark hinges on a curious conflation of national identity with national experience. For Ryan invests Clark with an insight into contemporary Australia that springs from Clark's historical

---

women, migrants — in other words anyone who is not an Anglo-Celtic male. While it is important to recognize the limitation of such a view of the forces that have given shape to Australian history as well as Australian identity, my point here is not to enter an argument with Clark's vision. I am more interested in the responses which his idiosyncratic style has provoked, and how such responses are linked to ways of representing Australian history.

54. *Manning Clark: Essays...*, p. 61.

55. *Manning Clark: Essays...*, p. 67.

vision, yet that vision is built on highly subjective idiosyncracies, which are subject to interpretation. Ryan would have profitted from reading Bakhtin's work on the epic and the novel, which clearly draws attention to the limitation of the epic as genre. Surely, first of all, all historians reflect the preoccupations of their contemporaneity in their explanations of how history 'has arrived'; and it is a characteristic that 'absolute epic distance separates the epic world from contemporary reality'[56], something which I would argue is precisely the case with Clark who, through his heavy-handed moralistic account, invests Australian history with a predetermined view more than any Australian historian, e.g. in the following brief extract:

> By the middle of February 1788 the secular and religious ceremonies to mark the beginning of the colony had been completed. Then the elementary task of housing, feeding, and preserving law and order was begun. In observing their behaviour in those early years when the foundations of civilization were hacked out in that rude and barbarous land, posterity has detected two patterns: how a settlement designed for the punishment and reformation of criminals developed within four days into a colony using convict labour, and how in transplanting a civilization changes quickly emerged in the character of that civilization. Such patterns escaped the minds of those on the spot. They were too preoccupied with the struggle for survival, dismayed by the difficulties of creating any civilization at all in such an alien environment and with such unpromising human material.[57]

While the epic traits are clear here in the sense of men engaging in mundane activities of greater significance than their collective actions, the question is naturally, what these activities are in the service of. The narration is not, as Ryan's conflation of history and national imagining might suggest, Australia's narrative, but the idiosyncratic vision of a historian who fails to take into account, all 'the lower orders', whether

---

56. Mikhail Bakhtin, *The Dialogic Imagination: Four Essays*, ed. by Michael Holquist (Austin: University of Texas Press), p. 13.

57. Manning Clark, *A History of Australia*, Vol. 1 (Melbourne: Melbourne U.P., 1962), p. 113.

they are convicts Aborigines, or women, and how they shaped their vision of Australia. Although Clark later addresses this as one of his omissions in his *History*, it is also true that, as Stuart Macintyre points out, 'the growing interest in class, gender and ethnicity as categories of historical interpretation posed particular problems for Clark's personification of the historical process'.[58] The incorporation of these groups into his account, which he attempts in the later volumes, not only exposes his eclective narrative style, as Macintyre also points out, they also undermine the historical space established by Clark's narrative frame, inside which Australian history can unfold. The question about Clark's historical practice, which considerations of his narrative style cannot render obsolete, opens a critical space for the intervention of historians, who raise at times quite damning critiques of Clark's practice. The review by M.H. Ellis, 'History without facts', which is reprinted in the volume on Clark, as well as John Barret's recount of R.W. Connell's dismissal of Clark's work, also in the Clark volume, are emblematic of this view. As Barret writes: 'With great slabs of material more or less lifted from insufficiently analysed documents, Clark's later work was damned by Connell as scissors-paste-history "raised to a high art"'.[59] This criticism hinges on an empirically based dismissal of Clark's *practice*. Other historians have engaged in a critique of Clark's *vision*, and that is more relevant in the context of my concerns here about the production of history.

One of the most profound attacks on Clark's historical vision, when he describes the beginning of the new settlement at Sydney, comes from Paul Carter, whose critique is summed up by Alan Atkinson:

> According to Carter, vol. I takes British power so much for granted that in spite of Clark's focus on events in Australia his work has to be seen as an example of 'imperial history'. It belongs to a type, which, by the method of its telling, creates 'the illusion of growing

58. Stuart Macintyre, 'Always a pace or two apart' in *Manning Clark: Essays…*, p. 25.
59. *Manning Clark: Essays…*, p. 115.

> purpose' as the central point of its narrative. As such, Carter says, 'it is wholly inadequate'; 'The primary object [of such work] is not to understand or to interpret: it is to legitimate.'[60]

Clark is not the only Australian historian Carter targets, but Clark's moralistic vision makes him particularly prone to attacks that expose the idiosyncratic nature of his vision. Carter's critique is not only directed at Clark's specific narrative style, but is part of a much more fundamental critique that draws attention to serious flaws in Clark's explanation models for historical processes. In a review of Carter's *The Road to Botany Bay,* the historian, Stuart Macintyre, lends support to Carter's challenge of Australian history writers by pointing out, what he sees as a pervasive problem in historical accounts of Australia's beginning:

> all of these efforts to write the history of exploration and settlement assume what they seek to explain. For all of them the country was there waiting to be found — (but) the assumption that historical space lay dormant waiting to be found robs it of its historical content.[61]

The anxiety to fill up the Australian space with meaning is clearly expressed in the unease surrounding the early chronological gaps in white Australian history. This manifests itself in two different ways. First, in the curious position granted to non-British exploration in Australia, that is, the unrecorded Chinese and Portuguese expeditions, the many recorded Dutch expeditions which mapped large sections of the Australian coastline, and the French scientific expeditions in the late eighteenth and early nineteenth centuries. Secondly, in the gaps in the almost exclusively British-Australian narration of early Australian history.

The earliest gap in British-Australian pre-settlement history is that between Dampier's visit to the northwest coast in the late seventeenth century and Cook's arrival on the east coast in 1770. Ironically, it is through Cook and the later British

60. *Manning Clark: Essays...*, pp. 128-29.

61. Macintyre quoted by George Seddon in 'On *The Road to Botany Bay*' in Westerly, no. 4, December 1988, p. 16.

penal colony that Dampier's visit is granted a significance, which in most historical accounts overshadows the far more extensive Dutch visits. However, the most unfortunate lapse is the chronological gap between Cook's departure in 1770 and Governor Phillip's arrival in 1788. In terms of Australia's judicial history this sense of misfortune (anxiety about the lack of continuity) has a great deal to do with the uncertainty about the nature and extent of the British claim on the continent. This in turn spills over into an as yet unresolved battle between two schools of Australian historians over the causes that led to the foundation of a British colony in Australia. Sources are dug out as supportive evidence on both sides, but what I find interesting here is not the details of this argument which has long since reached a stalemate. Rather it is their projection of a specific historical Australian space, for both schools in effect produce a closed reading of early colonial history, whose primary function is to reject the other reading, and as such their readings are both exclusivist. The two schools may be dubbed the 'navigation school' and the 'convict dumping ground school', but for my reading here, I find it more productive to look at them as the specific manifestations of the distinction, I established in the beginning of this Chapter between a conservative (imperialist) school and a radical (nationalist) school.

The discussion broke out in the 1960s between Geoffrey Blainey, representing the navigation school, and A.G.L. Shaw representing the convict school. It has continued to dominate Australian historiographical discourse. In the 1980s and 1990s Alan Frost has been one of the navigation school champions, while the convict school has been represented by Robert Hughes through his monumental study on Australia's convict origins, *The Fatal Shore*, published in 1987, on the eve of the Bicentennial. Although the heirs to the two schools may uncover new material in support of his school's argument, neither school has shifted their position since the debate began in the 1960s. Hence the main point of the navigation school remains that Australia became a colony primarily (or exclusively) because of its potential as a naval port for the British Empire. This school regards Sydney as an important location for controlling trade within, as well as to and from, the Pacific. It dedicates much attention to the flax and pines found on Norfolk Island, which it was thought, runs the argument, would replace existing suppliers in the volatile and enclosed Baltic states. It is central to the argument of the navigation school to assign a strategic importance to the Australian colony, which makes it an important investment for the Empire's strategic interests in the future. As the argument runs Australia would become, in the often quoted words by Governor Phillip, 'a most valuable acquisition' (though Phillip uses this argument in support of the land's agricultural potential, to ensure the continued attention from the colonial administrators in London). Geoffrey Blainey's Australian history book, *The Tyranny of Distance,* represents the most consistent effort to bring forth the arguments of this school. Blainey builds his thesis on overcoming distance as the concerted efforts of the Australian colonies, on reining in the too long umbilical cord between colonial periphery and metropolitan centre:

> The idea of distance throws new light on the rise of and importance of whaling, wool, gold and the dynamic export industries of the nineteenth century, on the immigration of Chinese in the 1850's and Italians a few decades later, and on immigration from the British Isles throughout Australian history. It illuminates the reasons why Australia was for long such a masculine society, why it became a more equalitarian society than North America, and why it was a relatively peaceful society.[62]

Blainey's comment makes it clear why the nature of Australia's beginnings is so hotly debated, for it is as if the way of giving birth to the colony determines once and for all the course of subsequent Australian history, and through this explains the evolution of an Australian identity. In this light the discussion is a reflection on the disagreement over Australia's contemporary make-up. The historians here cloud over the contemporary concerns, which inform their interpretation of the past through their preferential reading of selected details. This curious blindness towards the projection of the historian's

62. Geoffrey Blainey, *The Tyranny of Distance* (Melbourne: Sun Books, 1966), p. ix.

own contemporaneity onto the past, is what the Sri Lankan anthropologist, Bruce Kapferer, in his study of nationalism in Sri Lanka and Australia has described as a conflation between presentation (or 'real' experience) and representation (construction of experience).[63] Kapferer here takes issue with both the empiricist bend of historical practice, as well as with the construction of national identity and its process of sacrilising certain historical events, in the case of Australia, the Gallipoli campaign.[64]

As I mentioned before I have no wish to enter the details of the debate between the navigation school and the convict school. However, I do want to deconstruct the position of the latter school, because of its own identification as a progressive

---

63. Bruce Kapferer, *Legends of People, Myths of State* (London: Smithsonian Institute Press, 1998). In a comment on Kapferer's comparison of nationalist practice in Australia and Sri Lanka, Australian historian K.S. Inglis 'declared Australian myths to be true and Sri Lankan ones false' (Kapferer, p. xi). Kapferer takes point of departure in Inglis's comment to make the more general observation, that 'in their constructions of the significance of the events at Gallipoli in 1915, Australians make statements about how they conceive their own lived-realities' (Kapferer, p. xi).

64. It is not that I do not recognise the existence of critical readings of the Gallipoli legacy, such as Alan Seymour's play, *The One Day of the Year*, George Johnston's novel, *My Brother Jack*, and later interventions such as A.B. Facey's autobiography, *A Fortunate Life*, and Peter Weir's film *Gallipoli*, but these interventions have not had a wider impact on how cultural histories of Australia are produced. John Rickard's reading of the fortunes of the Anzac myth is revealing for its lack of awareness of the larger configurations of nationalist constructions inside which it operates: 'By the 1960s Anzac itself was under attack.... The attempts to develop another focus for national observance, as with Australia Day on 26 January...have met with yawns of indifference' (John Rickard, *Australia, a Cultural History* (London: Longman, 1988), pp. 220-21). Although Rickard's focus is on popular nationalism, that is arguably also a device for displacing concerns over nationalism from an academic environment. In Rickard's reading the post-war period paves the way for a shift from British-based hierarchical, values, to American-based materialist values, from an elite-based culture to a mass-based culture. Yet the Gallipoli myth escapes virtually intact, it remains sacrosanct regardless of the questions raised e.g. by Seymour's play. Furthermore, Rickard fails to identify what roles the cultural historians play in this process. How does Rickard place himself in relation to other schools of Australian historians?

school in opposition to a regressive conservative nationalism, a distinction with which I agree. It is precisely because of its self-proclaimed radical departure from a conservative nationalism that I find the convict school interesting to position in relation to the question of imposing limits on national identity formation in Australia. As mentioned before two of the most important champions of the school are A.G.L. Shaw and Robert Hughes. In the following paragraphs I will discuss their arguments, both in the light of the debate over the foundation of the first penal settlement and in relation to the reinterpretations and re-enactments which dominated the Australian Bicentennial in 1988.

Two points are central for A.G.L. Shaw's argument concerning the first settlers at Sydney Cove; one relates to the officers, the other to the convicts. In Shaw's representation of the officers and of the relations between the colonial and the metropolitan administrators it is clear that the metropolitan Englishmen pay insufficient attention to the difficulties faced by Governor Phillip, just as the officers create problems for a well-intentioned Phillip:

> The governor was more often hindered than helped by his second in command, Lieutenant-Governor Major Ross of the marines, described by one of his subordinates as 'without exception the most disagreeable commanding officer I ever knew'. Ross refused to allow his force to have anything to do with the convicts except to guard them. He objected to his men being subject in any way to the night watch which Phillip instituted in an attempt to reduce the thieving so prevalent in the settlement in the days of shortages; though the marines were not innocent of nocturnal plunderings. Ross would not have them interfered with by the well-behaved convicts who made up this primitive police-force.... Eventually Phillip managed to get rid of him by putting him in charge of Norfolk Island.... However, Phillip's patience, dignity and perseverance enabled him to lead the settlement successfully in its battle for survival.[65]

65. A.G.L. Shaw, '1788-1810' in *A New History of Australia*, ed. by F.K. Crowley (Melbourne: William Heinemann, 1974), p. 12.

In Shaw's reading here the governor's efforts to build up a colony are guided by common-sense and a practical view. Phillip's essentially well-intentioned work is thwarted by the petty behaviour of his junior officers. In this way Shaw criticises the hierarchical order among the British officers, but it is important to note that the governor is described as outside this pecking order, and Phillip might even be said to end up as an early prototype of the 'Aussie battler'.

The convicts on the other hand, one might expect to be idealised, since they are the egalitarian, anti-British authority stock from which future Australians descend, but Shaw's assessment of them is even-handed:

> Among all the convicts, political prisoners and those in any way respectable were few, and the idea that NSW was peopled by gallant radicals or starving unemployed is a myth — though like many myths it dies hard. Though no single simple description can do justice to some 160,000 prisoners during eighty years, most were a disreputable lot, poorly educated, young, urban ne'er-do-wells, with a virtually non-existent family life; two minority groups were 'atrocious villains'; and those hardly done-by, victims of injustice, or martyrs to their political or social beliefs. Of the last, nearly all came from Ireland.... They seem to have terrified both Governor Hunter and his successor...the authorities could be as ruthless, brutal and careless of legal proprieties in NSW as in Ireland itself.[66]

There is little suggestion of the future seeds of a triumphant egalitarian Australia stemming from Shaw's convicts. However, one would expect to find such sentiments expressed in another prominent representative of the radical school, Robert Hughes, in his book, *The Fatal Shore*. The book has all the trappings of a Bicentennial book. It was published on the eve of the Bicentennial, deals with the first white settlers, and has a monumental size as if to give the final verdict on Australia's European beginning. I will return to look at the Bicentennial in the light of the multicultural Australia which is also explored

---

66. A.G.L. Shaw, in *A New History of Australia*, pp. 22-23.

in the chapter dealing with multiculturalism and the Chinese-Australians. Here I am concerned with the more specific historical representations that were circulated during the Bicentennial. Hughes like Shaw starts on a note that does not seem to encourage a connection between the convicts and nation-building activities:

> The disappointing truth about Australia was that once the legend of the Southern Continent had been disproved and the facts about New Holland were known, there was not much reason to go there.[67]

The interesting point about Hughes is that, contrary to what is customary among Australian historians, he does not shy away from outlining his own position in opposition to other historiographical schools. The historical discourse is actually an integral part of his study, and he dedicates much effort to this debate. Hughes is necessarily sceptical of the merits of the navigation school, yet what is more interesting in the present context is his presentation of the navigation school's reasons for purporting their view:

> This vision of the embryo colony as 'a strategic outlier' of England, not just an opportunistically chosen dump for its criminals, has become popular with Australians as our national bicentenary approaches. It lends dignity to our beginnings. 'The rag and bone shop of Australia's beginning,' wrote the main spokesman for this view, Alan Frost, 'was perhaps not so foul as we have long supposed.' We shall see.[68]

Hughes' laconic statement has an almost too inviting boomerang effect, for while the desire for uplifting the view of Australia's beginning is understandable, if problematic due to its unrelativised perspective, why does Hughes find it necessary to do the opposite. Here the interest in the truth, or the no-nonsense approach of laying bare Australia's beginnings, is hardly sufficient. Yet, Hughes gives us no clues as to his own motivations here, nor as to how they might influence his personal vision. However, in the introduction

---

67. Robert Hughes, *The Fatal Shore* (London: Pan Books, 1988), p. 56.

68. Hughes, p. 56.

he does present a few clues as to what has propelled him to embark upon such a monumental journey:

> I realized that like nearly all other Australians I knew little about the convict past of my own country.... Convict history was ignored in schools and little taught in universities — indeed, the idea that the convicts might have a history worth telling was foreign to Australians in the 1950s and 1960s.... An unstated bias rooted deep in Australian life seemed to wish that 'real' Australian history had begun with Australian respectability.... Behind the bright diorama of Australia Felix lurked the convicts, some 160,000 of them, clanking their fetters in the penumbral darkness.[69]

While it is highly commendable in itself to draw attention to the poor convicts shamefully ignored by history, there is a problem in Hughes' project that perhaps becomes clearer when he indirectly describes the historical practice that informs his understanding of his subject:

> The missing element in most accounts of the System has been the voices of the convicts themselves.... This book is largely about what they tell us of their suffering and survival, their aspiration and resistance, their fear of exile and their reconciliation to the once-unimagined land they and their children would claim as their own.[70]

As in Shaw's account it would appear that we are engaged in looking for men, whose mundane activities betray the larger myth-making they are part of. Hughes has taken upon himself the role as an unproblematised mediator, the conveyor of thoughts from the past entered into the present unchanged, which would suggest that there is no historian's project of building up a particular universe, corresponding to a particular reading of Australia's beginning as a convict colony. Thus while Hughes's direct engagement with the motivations behind the navigation school's reading shows his understanding of the importance of representation, this insight is promptly ignored in relation to the polemical side of his own project.

69. Hughes, p. xi.

70. Hughes, p. xiv.

Hughes wants to persuade his readers to accept his version of early colonial history, but what he argues for is his successful replacement of an interested reading, with a disinterested, sampled recording of history, as if history can be simply transferred into the present.

Yet, it is clear even when Hughes is writing his own version of Australia's beginning that the navigation school is there as his shadow, his implied antagonistic reader. Hence Hughes directs his attention to the careful explanation of particular points that are only interesting in the context of the debate about Australia's colonial beginning. Probably no isolated incident has caused more debate than the gap of almost 18 years between Cook's visit in 1770 and Phillip's arrival in 1788, because the gap presents a British void in colonial Australia's beginning, and consequently a gap in the historical records. For the navigation school it is imperative that this gap be filled with English deliberations over how best to make use of the important discovery. Having decided that the discovery was important the navigation school needs to demonstrate the continuation of British interest. Hughes on the other hand uses the gap to show how the English showed no interest in Australia:

> Never had a colony been founded so far from its parent state, or in such ignorance of the land it occupied. There had been no reconnaisance. In 1770 Captain James Cook had made landfall on the unexplored east coast of this utterly enigmatic continent, stopped for a short while at a place named Botany Bay and gone north again. Since then, no ship had called: not a word, not an observation, for seventeen years, each one of which was exactly like the thousands that had preceded it, locked in its historical immensity of blue heat, bush, sandstone and the measured booming of glassy Pacific rollers.[71]

What emerges from Hughes's narrative here is a juxtaposition of that which is usually considered familiar/known, with that which is alien/unknown. For the description of the Australian bush and coast is a familiar one, since Australian nature continues unchanged through time spans, which are

71. Hughes, p. 1.

insignificant except in terms of human history. The scenery Hughes depicts is familiar to present-day Australians, and as such the English presence becomes an alienating interlude, between pre-colonial Australia and present-day Australians, who are bound to their location through their immediate recognition of Australian nature. As Hughes concludes, 'for its first forty years, everything that happened in the thief-colony was English'.[72]

So, from considerations of what created the Australian colonies in the first place, we have moved on to identify the process by which Australia becomes Australian. This is a process that is spatial and temporal at the same time. Temporal because Hughes links the evolution of an Australian identity either with the period after the first forty years of colonialism, or through a connection between pre-colonial Aboriginal Australia and the later emergence of an Australian identity. One example that illustrates this is the following quotation: 'On April 22, they saw some Australians on a beach. They looked black but it was hard to see their real color'.[73] Although it appears self-evident to say that Aborigines are Australians, it becomes a problematic statement in the light of the subsequent violent contact history between whites and Aborigines, where the white image of the Aborigines was premised on regarding Aborigines as inherently different from (white) Australians. In this period Aborigines failed to be Australians precisely because their presence as indisputably Australian disturbed the exclusive identification of white Australians as the continent's proper inhabitants. Hence it is not only, as Hughes implies, the British who fail to recognise the Aborigines as rightful owners, it is a view that continues to inform the position of Hughes's colonial and 'post-colonial' European-Australians. This is where Hughes's Australianness becomes spatial, because his ready inclusion of Aborigines as Australians presupposes a reading of an Australia, identified through a diversity of groupings (independently of time), rather than the trope of difference (created through both British and European-Australian colonialism). This spatialness at times

72. Hughes, p. 2.

73. Hughes, p. 53.

contradicts Hughes's temporal identification of Australianness as emerging out of the English colonial regime; for instance in the following description of the debauchery taking place when the first female convicts are taken ashore in 1788:

> It was the first bush party in Australia, with 'some swearing, others quarrelling, others singing....' And as the couples rutted between the rocks, guts burning from the harsh Brazilian *aguardiente*, their clothes slimy with red clay, the sexual history of colonial Australia may fairly be said to have begun.[74]

The specific description of the convicts' behaviour is consistent with popular images of how Australians behave today, but predates Hughes's own date for demarcating an Australian departure (this time according to Hughes's own schedule a 40 year gap). What I find more productive in Hughes's description is the way in which un-British things keep intruding into the narrative, such as supply ships from Asia, and in the case above, 'Brazilian aguardiente', images which open for questions concerning the straight-laced colonial periphery/ metropolitan centre bind that is reproduced by radical and conservative nationalists alike. Unfortunately, in Hughes account they are never fleshed out, but remain as shades indicating other less reductive colony-empire axis orientated explanations. What Hughes does pursue is a relentless demolition of Australia's early colonial years as a nation building activity:

> Some women prostituted themselves for a few handfuls of weevily flour or a hunk of gristle. Most of the men on the work gangs were already as naked as the Aborigines, having traded off their clothes for food. There was no question of the convicts' helping one another; Sydney Cove had only distilled the dog-eat-dog misery of the English slums.... The guards were as apathetic as the convicts.... The spirit of inquiry about the new environment, which had filled several officers' journals in the first year of settlement, now dwindled.... Monotony reigned. The classes were now at a simmering distrust

74. Hughes, p. 89.

> of one another, wrote an anonymous male convict lamenting their 'Crusoe-like adventures'.[75]

The idea of Australia as a prison creates not only a negative, but also an explanatory vacuum inside which the evolution of an Australian identity cannot be formed.[76] So, in the end Hughes selects a particular group which breaks away not only from the isolation of a British colonial prison, but who also in the same process literally catapult themselves into the bush and into Australian characters, the bushrangers:

> And so the absconder, by making the bush his new home, renamed it with the sign of freedom. On its blankness, he could inscribe what could not be read in spaces already colonized and subject to the laws and penal imagery of England.... By taking to the bush, the convict left England and entered Australia.[77]

Hughes here significantly selects a group that he locates outside the system he sees as a British intrusion into an already existing Australia that is more than anything produced by 'nature' (the Australian bush). Nature undermines the British regime and makes the Australians literally 'naturally Australian'. As in the navigation school accounts of Australia's colonial beginning what is interesting in Hughes's account is its omissions, those which his account is unable to include in his narration. Hence while Hughes resurrects a suppressed group to the status of heroes, and as such questions the navigation school's emphasis on continuity between Britain and its white colony, what gives shape to Australian identity in Hughes's historiography is a by-product of the inner

75. Hughes, p. 102.
76. The point I am making here is related to the question of whether national identity can be defined negatively. Frantz Fanon has pointed to the enabling colonial identification with that which has been cast by the white colonial oppressor as negative defining characteristics of the black person. However, the dilemma in the case of colonial Australia is that the whites are simultaneously colonisers and colonised. Arguably it is the double position of the white Australians which Hughes uses to advance a reading which creates a convenient division between the evil British and victimised but also self-emancipating colonial Australians.
77. Hughes, p. 243.

dialectics of the convict system. But in order to flesh out those absences, which are outside the empire-colony axis, it is necessary to turn to the Bicentennial and the discussions, which accompanied its acts of commemoration.

The Bicentennial

In his history of Australia, *Claiming a Continent*, David Day opens his account with the Bicentennial re-enactment of the arrival of the First Fleet on January 26, 1988. Day's opening is significant in itself, since it points to a continuous preoccupation with beginnings as a way of understanding Australia's evolving status as a nation. In his description of the Bicentennial Day points to the many, who celebrated the re-enactment, but also draws attention to the Aboriginal protesters, thus signalling two antagonistic responses to the Bicentennial, which illustrate the inherent contradictions of such an activity. As Day comments 'whether Phillip's landing constituted an act of invasion or merely of settlement became a matter of considerable historical and political debate'.[78] A perusal of the Bicentennial events and promotional material as well as subsequent readings of its staging reveals the year as a particularly intense manifestation of what Tom Nairn has called the nation as 'the modern Janus',[79] that is the idea of the nation imagining itself as simultaneously progressively future orientated and rooted in a primordial originating moment.[80] This juxtaposition is enabling for my reading of the Bicentennial here. 1988 may be viewed as a specific manifestation of nationalism producing the future as a projection of an insisted upon reading of the past. This is perhaps not so surprising. However, I would argue, that

78. David Day, *Claiming a Continent: A New History of Australia* (Sydney: HarperCollins, 1997), p. 454.

79. See his 'The Modern Janus', *New Left Review*, 94 (November-December, 1975).

80. Homi Bhabha discusses Nairn's statement and draws attention to the problematic marriage between nation and capitalism, progression and regression and rationality and irrationality. See Homi Bhabha's Introduction to *Nation and Narration* and his essay, 'Dissemination: Time, Narrative and the Margins of the Modern Nation', in *Nation and Narration* (London: Routledge, 1990).

nationalism also produces the past through an insisted upon reading of the future. Both processes then are products of a struggle over the meaning of the nation's present. In the case of the Australian Bicentennial this struggle is manifest in the debate over what constituted an appropriate bicentennial event. This is a rather ill disguised struggle for control over the meaning of the nation, displaced through arguments over the appropriate forms of national representation and more specifically over the re-enactment of the colonial beginning. The celebration of certain links (back to the convicts rather than officers, white rather than black, monocultural rather than multicultural) over others and the overt containment of the endorsed spectre of representations of the past, confirms the Bicentennial was an operation in ideological containment of the future, through the control over the interpretation of the past. The commemoration/celebration thus represents a different exercise from historical accounts of the colonial beginning, because a displacement through a narrativisation of the historical source material does not take place, the ramifications for contemporary readings of Australian society are much more immediate. In *Illusions of Identity,* Anne-Marie Willis neatly sums up the dilemmas and contradictions involved in setting up the Bicentennial:

> As a projected celebration of 200 years of nationhood, it faced a number of contradictions. Narratives of white progress were no longer universally supported.... Yet the desire for the celebration of an historical moment which could be figured as the founding moment of nation was present among sectors of the Anglo population.
>
> This partially thwarted desire was manifested in two ways: a private venture, a First Fleet Re-enactment Voyage; and the official and much more vague 'Tall ships' project. To officially endorse a re-enactment would have been politically unacceptable; instead this was gestured to by evoking heritage in the romantic figure of tall ships which sailed into Sydney Harbour on Australia Day 1988. Interestingly this was an idea taken directly from the American Bicentenary of 1976.
>
> The second problem faced was the discourse of multiculturalism which had been receiving increasing

> official endorsement in the years leading up to the Bicentenary. At one stage the official Bicentennial theme was to be 'Living Together', acknowledging the nation's multicultural heritage. Then 'The Australian Achievement' was floated. Eventually, the less controversial theme of 'Celebration of a Nation' was adopted and the event was conceived of as a year-long party. Aboriginal and multicultural demands succeeded in toning down the Anglo-centrism of the official face of the Bicentenary.[81]

In 1992 *Celebrating the Nation: A Critical Study of Australia's Bicentenary* was published.[82] It brought together a collection of essays dedicated to the scrutiny of various aspects of the Bicentenary. Yet one curious absence is history, bar two essays which both speak of the role played by constructions of history in the official activities. No article takes up the challenge of revisiting the colonial site of contention. Although other essays are critical readings of the choices made by the organisers in their representations of the nation, it is Peter Cochrane and David Goodman's article 'The Great Australian Journey' which most productively shows how the past is in effect mirrored in the preoccupations of contemporary Australia. This approach is neatly encapsulated in their comment that 'rarely, it must be said, has so much attention in Australia been directed towards, or so much effort been expended on, a battle for symbolic authority in representing the past'.[83] Their article presents an interesting departure for connecting the representations of the past with the concerns of the present, and as such paves the way for opening new avenues for exploring Australian colonial beginnings.

Cochrane and Goodman devote much space in their article to the dilemmas faced by the Bicentennial authority, which was trapped by the fact that 'too much stress on the first settlement was clearly divisive, too little, and the obvious

---

81. Anne-Marie Willis, *Illusions of Identity: The Art of a Nation* (Sydney: Hale & Iremonger, 1993), p. 177.

82. *Celebrating the Nation: A Critical Study of Australia's Bicentenary*, ed. by Tony Bennett, Pat Buckridge, David Carter and Colin Mercer (Sydney: Allen & Unwin, 1992).

83. *Celebrating the Nation*, p. 177.

question arose: why pick 1988?'[84] Cochrane and Goodman go on to detail the development in the Bicentennial agenda and its political manoeuvring, concluding that the preparations were haunted by an ideological anxiety which resulted in 'a shift in emphasis from the voyage of the First Fleet, to *all* the voyages of arrival to Australia, to all the 'people who have settled this land over many thousands of years'.[85] This shift to an all-embracing Australian experience (particularly when it is extended 50,000 years into the past to accommodate the arrival of the Aborigines) produces an altered focus on the 'theme of the journey, an abstraction of the immigration experience'.[86] Unfortunately, it also essentially makes all arrivals equal, hence displacing the issue of invasion and the unequal migrant status (free settlers vs. convicts, the White Australia policy, the widely criticised migrant detention centres after World War II, and so on). In Cochrane and Goodman's words the all-embracing approach leads to 'the erasure of difference, of time, and of power and domination'.[87]

At the surface level the bicentennial dilemma was that on the one level the commemoration/celebration reached back to the beginning of colonial Australia, while on the other the Bicentennial was inevitably caught up in making statements about contemporary Australia. It would be tempting to argue that this dilemma was due to colonial Australia's lacking relevance for a contemporary, multicultural Australia. This, however, is to see bicentennial Australia only in the light of an ahistorical, progressive modernity. It is as important to remember that the inconsistencies in the bicentennial commemoration cannot be separated from Australian historiography's preference for a British-Irish narrative history, according to which a nation already formed by settlement, has gradually accommodated a multicultural reality, particularly from the 1960s and 1970s when the last barriers of the White Australia policy were dismantled. This reading follows official multicultural policy, which grants a contemporary space to a

84. *Celebrating the Nation*, p. 177.
85. *Celebrating the Nation*, p. 178.
86. *Celebrating the Nation*, p. 178.
87. *Celebrating the Nation*, p. 178.

spectre of cultures, on largely ahistorical terms. The definition of Australian identity historically is already given through the insistence on defining its past as settlement history, regardless of Australia's long multicultural history, and through a sanitised view of white-black relations. While individual histories of Australia may mention a long tradition of multicultural presences in Australia, perhaps most notably the Chinese, they have been at pains to point out the negligible influence of such presences on the part of Australian history that is seen as formative for an evolving Australian identity. Much as the continued struggle between Aborigines and white settlers on the frontier is reduced to regrettable but isolated regional incidents.

The Bicentennial's emergence as a nation-building activity, its keywords of 'celebration' and 'achievement' and its eagerness to include all Australians without challenging received Australian history brought on a focus on the nation's contemporaneity. This in turn paved the way for new critical assessments of its history, because of the evident historical inconsistencies between the traditional version of peaceful Anglo-Australian settlement on the one hand, and the fact of the invasion and Australia's much longer and stronger multicultural history than acknowledged, on the other.

David Goodman's 'Postscript 1991' follows a similar vein, when he reflects upon the implications of the contradictions over appropriate representational forms of the nation as a contemporary configuration during the Bicentennial:

> The images circulated and displayed in the course of the various Bicentennial events enacted solutions to ideological dilemmas about national representation. The journey, the spectacle, the panorama became the characteristic forms of a powerful impulse to a form of symbolic inclusiveness which characterised the official celebrations. On the eve of the Bicentennial year David Burchell pondered how it was that, with so many 'progressive people' involved in work on aspects of the Bicentennial programme it appeared in the end as only 'a hotch potch of therapeutic devices interspersed with gestures towards cultural diversity and racial

> reconciliation'. How was it that critical ideas proved so ineffective?[88]
>
> The deeper answer surely lies with the kinds of critiques available: specifically, the legacy of those critiques of earlier unitary definitions of the Australian nation which consisted mainly of pointing to diversity and to those who were 'left out' or marginalised by dominant versions of Australian history and self-definition...there are limits to the grip that critiques which are just about inclusion can have. For new official pluralist ideologies in Australia easily incorporate such critical discourses as part of a depiction of the nation as a happy diversity, a mobile postmodern collage of difference.[89]

At the heart of Goodman's critique lies the particular form of multiculturalism which 'Australia' as a nation has embraced, even if some have done it more reluctantly than others. I will explore this particular brand of multiculturalism further in a later Chapter, but for now merely point out that the eagerness with which new 'cultures' are embraced betrays the anxiety-ridden status of Australian multiculturalism. It shows how current Australian multicultural practice suffers from its inability to effectively challenge the foundation of the older forms of national identity. Australian multiculturalism merely strives to be all-inclusive pointing to the obvious redundancy of former narrow exclusivist models, but fails to recognise that although models may be redundant, the privileges which such models supported, may continue in an apolitical multicultural practice. Goodman's argument follows a similar vein when he reiterates the argument pursued in *Mistaken Identity: Multiculturalism and the Demise of Nationalism in Australia*[90] on the limitations of a multiculturalism that seeks to antagonise no one. However, Goodman then takes issue with the desire in *Mistaken Identity* to nonetheless try to define an Australian quality within the new multicultural

88. *Celebrating the Nation*, p. 192.
89. *Celebrating the Nation*, pp. 192-93.
90. *Mistaken Identity: Multiculturalism and the Demise of Nationalism in Australia*, ed. by Stephen Castles, Mary Kalantzis, Bill Cope and Michael Morrissey (Sydney: Pluto Press, 1988).

tradition. Arguably then, the problems involved in a new multicultural approach is more about the limitations imposed on the new than the fight against redundant models of Anglo-Australian citizenship evolving in the bush. Goodman quotes Paul James who has argued:

> that the postmodern critique of nationalism was complicit with the openness brought about by the internationalisation of capital and the 'dissolution of the old, closed national form'. He noted further the changed quality of contemporary nationalism, its 'more open, abstract' character. Gerry Gill has written similarly of the 'current enchantment with openness' which 'does not distinguish between the genuinely liberating and the emergence of a new order of domination which requires the dissolution of the older structures and boundaries'. This kind of argument has still not received the attention it deserves in Australian cultural studies, preoccupied as they often are with either the defence or the critique of the older unitary definitions of the Australian nation.[91]

The answer to this dilemma is presumably the development of a far more radical critique not only of the operation of Australian multiculturalism, but also of how that multiculturalism, through its desire to maintain consensus, in effect extends the disparities of the old nationalist models through an adjustment/expansionist model. This exercise is problematic precisely because the older nationalist models are premised on the suppression of the fact of white invasion and the historiographic denial of a longer multicultural history, which not only existed but also influenced and indeed in important ways determined the shaping of Australian history.

At the other end of the scale an Australian multiculturalism which defines the nation through a shifting consensus within a progressive state, also leaves certain segments of the established Anglo-Australian order behind, while upgrading particular upwards mobile segments of migrant communities from other parts of the world to power-brokering citizens. While this is certainly true it is equally revealing that these

91. *Celebrating the Nation*, p. 196.

economically marginalised sectors of the Anglo-Australian community are still in a position to identify and suppress marginalised communities at least as far as the participation in espousing national values is concerned. The Asian-Australians and the Aborigines have been the favoured targets of the new right in Australia, and continue to be so, regardless of the fact that smaller segments of their communities (by other parts of the Australian society) may have been elevated as success stories of entrepreneurial migrants, or Aborigines who have broken the vicious circle of poverty, abuse and discrimination. A new critical positioning in relation to both 'singular' and 'pluralistic' nationalisms in Australia need to take on board a historical reassessment of the multicultural contribution to an Australian identity. This positioning follows Graeme Turner's argument that new critical readings of Australian nationalism 'understand nationalism itself as an oppressively consensualising ideology'[92] and that 'national cultures are to be approached as sites of contestation in which competition over definitions takes place'.[93] Turner's reading is instrumental for my reading in the following chapters on Australian cultural history in the light of its relation with both an internalised and an external Asia.

REFERENCES

A New History of Australia, ed. by F.K. Crowley (Melbourne: William Heinemann, 1974).

Beaglehole, J.C. (ed.), *The Endeavour Journal of Joseph Banks 1768-1771*, Vols. 1 and 2 (Sydney: Angus & Robertson, 1962).

Beaglehole, J.C. (ed.), *The Journals of Captain Cook on his Voyages of Discovery* (Cambridge: Hakluyt Society, 1955-74).

Blainey, Geoffrey, *The Tyranny of Distance* (Melbourne: Sun Books, 1966).

Bolton, Geoffrey, *Who Owns Australia's Past?* (St. Lucia, Qld: UQP, 1993).

Carter, Paul, *The Road to Botany Bay* (London: Faber, 1987).

Celebrating the Nation: A Critical Study of Australia's Bicentenary ed. by Tony Bennett, Pat Buckridge, David Carter and Colin Mercer (Sydney: Allen & Unwin, 1992).

Clark, Manning, *A History of Australia, vol. 1* (Melbourne: Melbourne U.P., 1962).

---

92. Graeme Turner, *Making It National: Nationalism and Australian Popular Culture* (Sydney: Allen & Unwin, 1994), p. 7.

93. *Making It National*, p. 10.

Crawford, R.M. et al., *Making History* (Melbourne: 1985).

Dallas, K.M., *Trading Post or Penal Colonies* (Melbourne: Fuller Bookshop, 1969).

Day, David, *Claiming a Continent: A New History of Australia* (Ryde, Sydney: HarperCollins, 2001).

Farrell, Frank, *Themes in Australian History: Questions, Issues and Interpretation in an Evolving Historiography* (Kensington, NSW: NSW University Press, 1990).

Fletcher, Brian, *A Passion for the Past: Writers of Australian History in New South Wales 1900-1938* (Sydney: Royal Australian Historical Society, 1990).

Fletcher, Brian, *Australian History in New South Wales 1888 to 1938* (Kensington, NSW: NSW University Press, 1993).

Frost, Alan, *Botany Bay Mirages* (Melbourne: Melbourne University Press, 1994).

Griffiths, Tom, *Hunters and Collectors: The Antiquarian Imagination in Australia* (Melbourne: Cambridge U.P., 1996).

Robert, Hughes, *The Fatal Shore* (London: Pan Books, 1988).

Kapferer, Bruce, *Legends of People, Myths of State* (London: Smithsonian Institute Press, 1998).

Macintyre, Stuart, *The Discovery of Australian History* (1890-1939).

Manning Clark: Essays on His Place in History, ed. by Carl Bridge (Melbourne: Melbourne U.P., 1994).

Martin, Stephen, *A New Land: European Perceptions of Australia 1788-1850* (Sydney: Allen & Unwin, 1993).

Mistaken Identity: Multiculturalism and the Demise of Nationalism in Australia, ed. by Stephen Castles, Mary Kalantzis, Bill Cope and Michael Morrissey (Sydney: Pluto Press, 1988).

Rickard, John, *Australia, a Cultural History* (London: Longman, 1988).

Seddon, George, 'On *The Road to Botany Bay*' in *Westerly*, no. 4, December 1988, pp. 15-26.

Shaw, A.G.L., *Convicts and the Colonies* (London: Faber, 1966).

Shaw, A.G.L., '1788-1810', in *A New History of Australia*, ed. by F.K. Crowley (Melbourne: William Heinemann, 1974), pp. 1-44.

Tench, Watkin, *1788 Comprising a Narrative of the Expedition to Botany Bay and A Complete Account of the Settlement at Port Jackson*, ed. and introduced by Tim Flannery (Melbourne: The Text Publishing Company, 1996).

Willis, Anne-Marie, *Illusions of Identity: The Art of a Nation* (Sydney: Hale & Iremonger, 1993).

2

Towards an Aboriginal-Asian Colonial Contact History

In the very beginning when the earth is still covered with water, Ned Kelly arrives at the Northern Territory in a boat. Like Noah — though it is not clear whether the storyteller made the parallel explicit — he sees a leaf and realises there is dry land. He and his band of angels go about shooting police. They also teach the Aborigines to make tea and cook damper, and there is feeding of the multitude that reminds us of the New Testament. The police eventually catch and hang him, but on the third day he emerges from the grave and with a great noise and shake of the earth he flies up into the sky.

Jeremy Beckett, 'Aboriginal Histories, Aboriginal Myths: An Introduction', *Oceania*, vol. 65, no. 2, p. 109

We liked the Macassans. They brought us many things. They came here for many years, and you can see where they got their water at the Macassan Well. That is the place where the tamarind trees are. (Tom Djawa, interview with Keith Cole at Milingimbi)

Art from the Land: dialogues with the Kluge-Ruhe Collection of Australian Aboriginal Art, ed. by Howard Morphy and Margo Smith Boles (Charlotteville: Uni of Virginia, 1991), p. 88

The two opening quotations both stem come from Aboriginal sources, they are both from Australia's tropical north, and they are both fragments of oral histories. The former may be described as internal in relation to Australian national history, in so far as it recapitulates (albeit in a fashion that also 'reoralises'), in a single narrative strand, some of the most central myths of Australian national history. By the same token the latter is external, because it deals with Aboriginal contacts abroad, which are conventionally regarded as outside the national history.[94] Even if colonial histories devote much attention to the importance of shipping, visiting Macassan fishermen connote the wrong kind of contact; attention is far more eagerly paid to the 'tyranny of distance' variety which confirms the umbilical cord between Australian colonial periphery and British imperial centre. Indeed, the umbilical

94. Even if in recent histories of Australia the trepang contact zone has begun to feature more prominently this phenomenon is still seen as peripheral and of no consequence for Australian history. Arguments for the dismissal of its significance include its limited time span and the lack of source material. To be fair some critique of this position has emerged e.g. in the earlier work of C.C. Macknight. Here is an illustrative comment from his book, *The Farthest Coast*:

> Australia's first modern industry was trepang. It was conducted by brown-skinned Muslims on the coast which is still among the loneliest in the world. The present pattern of Australian development has obscured these facts, so that many are surprised by the diversity of the continent's history. This book...aims to increase awareness of that diversity. (Macknight, p. 1)

Macknight, however, has little to say concerning the reasons for this lack of diversity. My argument is that the point is not so much about diversity, as it is about difference. Aboriginal-Macassan contact history does not merely add to a diversification of Australian history, it challenges the monothematic narrative of settlement history. This becomes clear if this phase in colonial history is not merely seen in isolation through a conventional episodic 19th century narration, but instead is linked to the modern nation's project of narrating its own arrival through its construction of particular histories, a kind of mapping backwards through time. The trepang trade does not suit the settlement narratives of European-Australian expansion from colonial beach heads (although settlements were attempted from the 1820s, it was only in the 1860s that a permanent settlement was established). In a mid-nineteenth century history of Australia, the trepang trade would have featured far more prominently, because it was seen as lucrative, and continued to be regarded in this light throughout that century. The contact between Aborigines and Macassans disturbs the narrative of a neatly isolated continent inhabited by a homogenised primitive people, whose dispossession of their continent can be explained as a unified and unifying take over.

cord is an insistence on a domestic relationship, which exists in spite of the wide 'dark tunnel' that must be crossed *en route*. The Macassan-Aboriginal contact zone is disturbing to national history construction in at least three different ways. First, it destroys the idea of Australia's supreme cultural isolation prior to the first settlement, which is important to the implicit understanding of a dynamic European culture inevitably replacing a static Aboriginal culture. Secondly, it draws attention to Australia's proximity to Asia, that is that the northern parts of Australia lay within a sphere of Asian interest and influence. Thirdly, the evidence that contacts took place for a long time beyond the reach of the colonial administration in southern Australia betrays the colonisation as a process of total containment of the indigene and monopolising of trade for the colonial state. This becomes manifest later on through the colonial administration's preoccupation with extending its territorial control to encompass the entire continent's periphery. The process of containing the continent first within the colonial administrations of the different territories and later on within the Australian federation culminates with the patrolling of the waters along the Australian north coast, which effectively puts a stop to the Aboriginal-Macassan trade and contact.

What I have been arguing, to return to the opening quotations, is that the separation of internal and external histories hinges on the acceptance of a geopolitical boundary, which was not in place through most of the period during which Aboriginal contact with Macassan fishermen[95] took place. Furthermore, the 'reoralised' bushranger story of Ned Kelly story originates from Australia's far south-eastern corner, and can hardly be more central to the locals than the annual visits from the Macassan fishermen that had taken place for generations. Thus the presence of the Ned Kelly which in one context can be read as an instance of indigenisation/ creolisation of a white settler myth, may in a geopolitical

95. For a more detailed history on who these Macassan fishermen/traders were, see Christian Pelras, *The Bugis* (London: Blackwell, 1996). The term Macassan refers to the fact that they came from the area around the present day seaport of Ujung Pandang, South Sulawesi.

context be read as evidence of the nation's intrusion into its border zones to assert its territorial claim through the identification of a shared mythology. Only through the insistence on the territorial integrity of Australia, the identification of an island/continent with a nation, can the connection between a Northern Territory oral history and a hero from the national narrative become 'naturalised'.

As I have already hinted at, the former story may, if approached from a different angle, also be said to be national in scope, while the latter is localised. Hence the former can be represented as an indigenisation of received Australian nationalist mythology, in the shape of Ned Kelly and the Bible, two cornerstones in the nation's narrative, even if they are quite often in mainstream Australian cultural histories produced as opposites. For Christianity has been linked, most famously by Manning Clark, with the creation of civilisation and order in an Australian wilderness, while Ned Kelly represents an anti-authoritarian myth, whose primary purpose is to draw attention to the repressiveness fundamental to Clark's civilisational order. Finally, both myths are also, from a localised northern Australian perspective, imposed narratives from afar. As such they show the Australian-British axis has been replaced by a different periphery-centre axis and that the new axis may be seen as an instance of a different 'tyranny of distance' thesis from the one Blainey pursued. It is useful to recapitulate that Blainey operates with a model of a shrinking distancing between Australia and its 'natural' parent culture due to an improvement of shipping technology, which has the curious effect of linking Australia closer with Britain over time. For Blainey the argument serves to 'naturalise' the status of Australia's privileged Anglo-phone elite. The connection between settlement narratives from the southeast and oral Aboriginal history in Australia's north represents, on the nation's behalf, a similar retrospective forging between periphery and centre in a process aimed at national unification. The process is not only narrative, of course, but finds a physical historical parallel in the manoeuvres aimed at bringing that border zone, which reminds the nation of its fragile historical hold on its edges, under the control/patrolling eye of the nation.[96]

Such manoeuvrings in Australia's north are evident from the colonial period and throughout Australia's history as an independent nation.[97] The early stages in this process can be seen in the mapping of the trade potential, which is set in motion after the continent has been circumnavigated by Matthew Flinders. Settlements and trading posts are established to cash in on the trepang trade, but tropical diseases and Aboriginal resistance stalls the colonisation process. Darwin is eventually set up, but the nation's decisive intrusion occurs with the patrolling of the northern coastal waters. In the narrative of one of these patrolling men, Alfred Searcy's *In Australian Tropics*, it becomes apparent how the economic desire to take over the profitable existing trade is inseparable from the activity of installing a physical border through economic means against existing traders:

> So long as this portion of the coast was waste there was no reason why the Malays should not gather the annual harvest and turn it to their own profitable account. But now that there was some chance of Europeans following

---

96. Of course this may also be spoken of in terms of internal neo-colonialism. Taking away the Aborigines' trading partners made them dependent on European goods and prices, and represented a step in the direction of turning them into what many Aborigines became; an unpaid labour force. On the Macassan side a parallel history can be traced. Hence the trepang fishing off Australia's north coast began when the Dutch monopolised trade with the eastern islands in the Indonesian archipelago, and the Macassans were forced to look elsewhere for economic survival. The Macassan trepang fishing ends when the Dutch monopolise trade out of Sulawesi. As on the Australian side economics are inseparable on the Indonesian side from the territorial ambitions of the colonial Dutch administration. Hence Indonesia was in the process of being made into a proper colonial state, as opposed to a string of separate colonial administrative units. This process, however, came to an end with the Japanese occupation during World War II and the Indonesian independence war after World War II.

97. One recent example is the Australian government's decision in 2002 not to recognise asylum seekers as having arrived in Australia, when they land on isolated islands and reefs over which Australia claim jurisdiction. The idea of actually surrendering sovereignty over the islands and reef doesn't feature in the government's calculations.

> suit, and with the idea of encouraging local trading on the coast, it was decided that the time had come for the Malays to be placed on an equal footing with the local people, and to pay something towards the revenue of the country, to which hitherto they had not contributed a penny, although they had removed from the coast millions of pounds' worth of spoil in the shape of trepang, pearls, pearl-shell, tortoise-shell, and timber.[98]

Searcy's choice of words is revealing here. The idea of the 'coast' lying 'waste' symbolically overwrites any meaningful Aboriginal activities in the area. 'Local trade' refers to the recent arrival in the area of the Europeans, who Searcy sees as candidates to take over the existing trade between Macassans and Aborigines.[99] It is as such another process of dispossession that is taking place, and one that is matched by the Dutch in Indonesia, through their restrictions on Macassan fishermen's activities in order to monopolise trade on the Dutch side of the Arafura Sea. To see the European-Australians as locals is contingent on the recognition of the territorial inclusion of the whole continent under white Australian jurisdiction, regardless of the paltry level of white presence in any particular area.

During these early patrolling years the Northern Territory is administered by, first the colony, and then the state of South Australia. The federal government takes over the charge

98. Searcy Alfred, *In Australian Tropics* (George Robertson, Sydney, 1909), p. 13.

99. To give but one example of the shifting 'white' priorities in the region, G. Earl's *Enterprise in Tropical Australia* (London: Madden and Malcolm, 1846) reveals a much higher priority granted by European-Australians to the economic potential of Macassan-Aboriginal cultural contact, as well as a lack of awareness about any 'Asian menace':

> [The Aborigines] have acquired the rudiments of commerce, and although the cultivation on the soil has not yet been attempted, they have learned to collect the natural productions of the country, with the view to exchanging them for food of a superior quality to that which their own land affords. A considerable number have paid one or more visits to Macassar, residing there for months together, which has familiarized them with the language and manners of the people of that country, and may probably lead to a closer intercourse, *should the Macassars establish themselves upon the coast.* (p. 118, my italics)

of the Northern Territory in 1911, after registering its unhappiness with the South Australian inability to populate the Northern Territory. Behind the federal irritation over the South Australian inaction lies an anxiety over the lack of control over the tropical north. This attitude betrays both a fear of an insufficiently guarded north (against the 'Asian hordes') as well as an urge to satisfy the nation's demand for control over its entire territory, and particularly over its border zones, which it systematically closes off to 'outsiders' after its own assertion of control. In this process it simultaneously encloses its internalised other (the Aborigines, whose alternative means of existence are cut off), and excludes its externalised other (the Asians, here in the shape of the Macassan traders). The two groups highlight the nation's unsettling awareness of its uncharted geopolitical territory. Any established practice of cultural exchange beyond the control of the federal administration[100] acts as a troubling reminder of the limitations of the tunnel vision approach to Australian colonial history writing's almost exclusive focus on European settlement history. The traditional patriarchal reading which begins with Cook's visit and continues with a host of British colonial representatives laying claim to a continent inhabited by easily dismissed primitive peoples is a particularly problematic approach. Even if one were to accept that a primitive state grants permission to invade and colonise, the long established alternative contact zone between what are in fact two colonised peoples[101] shows a far more complex trade pattern than what

100. The extent and sophistication of the trade is clear from Searcy's following comment:

> I made preparations for my first voyage down the coast to warn the masters of the proas that in future a licence would have to be paid, and also duty on the stores used on the coast. The stores consisted of rice, arrack, and tobacco, great quantities of which were tendered to the natives in the way of barter and for help rendered in the trepanging operations. (Searcy, pp. 13-14)

101. A much more detailed colonial contact history between Macassans and Aborigines could be carried out here. On the Indonesian side one would have to look at the ways in which the Dutch colonial regime asserted its control over its colonial subject by monopolising trade, indeed in a similar move to what happened on the Australian side. To look at connections during Australia's colonial period would entail an

would support the idea of a primitive nomadic people. To legitimate invasion it is necessary to dismiss all evidence of alternative dynamic cultural interchange.

Australian settlement histories have relegated Aboriginal histories to the margins along with non-British migrant histories and women's histories. Annette Hamilton has drawn attention to how such similar practices of exclusion and strategic inclusions operate in Australian cultural histories to produce 'Aborigines and Asians', suggesting 'that the deep ambivalence towards these "imagined communities" stems from their positions respectively at the "empty heart" and "fragile boundaries" of the Australian consciousness'.[102] She elaborates on this separation of Aborigines and Asians from mainstream Australian concerns and suggests that they in effect reveal an 'un-settledness' at the heart of nationalist settlement discourse. In Hamilton's reading the explanation for the experience of Aborigines and Asians as a disturbing presence is not to be found in psychological approaches to nationalist discourse, but through the post-colonial trope of appropriation:

> Although there is fear of something in the heart and outside the boundaries, there is also a lure and a fascination, which can be neutralised not by retreat but by appropriation. This is not an appropriation of 'the real': it is an appropriation of commodified images, which permits the Australian national imaginary to claim certain critical and valuable aspects of 'the Other' as essentially part of itself, and thereby claim both a mythological and spiritual continuity of identity which is otherwise lacking.[103]

If such an internal repression of the histories of those on the margins of the nation is due to the challenge they pose to conventional representations of Australian history, we need

---

exploration of the imperial-colonial axis on the Dutch-Indonesian and the British-Australian side.

102. Annette Hamilton, 'Fear and Desire': Aborigines, Asians and the National Imaginary, pp. 14-35, p. 18, in *Australian Perceptions of Asia. Special Issue of Australian Cultural History*, no. 9, 1990 ed. by David Walker, Julian Horne and Adrian Vickers.

103. Hamilton, p. 18.

to look elsewhere to begin to find evidence of how an alternative representation of Australian history may be constructed through the attentive focus on the margins of the national territory.

Australian anthropology has a long established preoccupation with the contact zones in its north, particularly between Arnhem Land Aborigines and Macassan fishermen on the one side, and between Torres Strait Islanders and Papua New Guinean peoples on the other:

> The Torres Strait has long held a special place in anthropology and archaeology due to its strategic position between the Australian and Papua New Guinean mainlands and A.C. Haddon's 1898 Cambridge Anthropological Expedition. For the most part, research interests have been directed towards documenting the selective diffusion of so-called higher cultural traits of 'advanced' Papuans to their 'primitive' Aboriginal neighbours across the Torresian divide.... These views gave rise to the concept of The Torres Strait as a 'cultural filter' for, or 'cultural barrier' to, material cultural traits.[104]

It is easy to see how such an approach was informed by preconceived notions of a hierarchy of cultures organised according to a trickling down effect from more sophisticated cultures from north to south. As such it belies an awareness of the anthropologist's own geographical location, and speaks in terms of degrees of difference from the culture of the anthropological self. There is little controversy in stating the Western bias of earlier anthropologists, who were instrumental in the process of establishing a colonial and later neo-colonial order around the world.[105] Where it becomes interesting is when one asks the question what has been learned from this

---

104. Ian J. McNiven, 'Enmity and Amity: Reconsidering Stone-headed Club (*gabagaba*) Procurement and Trade in Torres Strait,' *Oceania*, vol. 69, pp. 94-115, p. 94.

105. See Adam Kuper, *The Invention of Primitive History* (London: Routledge, 1988), Robert Young, *Colonial Desire: Hybridity in Theory, Culture and Race* (London: Routledge, 1995) and Peter Hulme, *Colonial Encounters: Europe and the Native Caribbean 1492-1797* (London: Routledge, 1986), pp. 54-57.

lopsided history and whether this has led to different approaches to understanding Aboriginal and Torres Strait Islander cultures?[106]

That anthropologists have been engaged in problematising 'naturalised' settlement histories is clear from Bain Attwood's assessment of the work by one of the anthropological authorities on indigenous culture, John Mulvaney. Attwood argues that Mulvaney's work:

> can be spoken of in terms of a challenge 'to the saga of conventional Australian history, which emerged during the closing years of the nineteenth and the opening decades of the next [which] served to authorize the seizing of the continent by presenting a history that only *began* when Europeans landed on these shores...creating a myth of an empty land'.[107]

However, although the excavation of such a history has the potential of unsettling received ideas of Australia's history, it

106. Few anthropologists concern themselves with the wider implications of their infatuation with the border-zone cultures, to which they declare themselves so drawn. This is but one example of a general reluctance to come to terms with a critique against the discipline that has been quite damning in its scope. The Introduction to John Mulvaney and Johan Kamminga's *Prehistory of Australia* (Sydney: Smithsonian Institution Press, 1999) is an instructive example. Although Mulvaney and Kamminga draw attention to the critique raised against their discipline (which they label archaeology, although clearly anthropology is deeply embedded in many sections of their book), they explicitly refuse to engage with the critique: 'We do not dwell on methods in Australian archaeology, nor explore in detail the important role of theory in interpreting archaeological data' (p. xvi). Nicholas Thomas in *Possessions: Indigenous Art/Colonial Culture* has one reference (p. 197) to anthropology's unfortunate marriage with colonialism: 'The criticism of anthropology became most vigorous only after the discipline had largely shifted away from an emphasis on tribal societies, and ceased to be blind to the ramifications of colonial histories....' It would appear that the problem has been shifted from the shoulders of the anthropologist to those of his/her critic. Whether that in any way results in a coming to terms with not only anthropology's engagement with colonial history, but also the legacy of that history remains an unanswered question.

107. Tim Bonyhady and Tom Griffiths (eds.), *Prehistory to Politics: John Mulvaney, the Humanities and the Public Intellectual* (Melbourne UP, 1996), Bain Attwood, Chapter 6, pp. 98-116; p. 99.

can also as I have discussed in other contexts in this book serve to legitimise the predominant view through an unproblematised expansion of the nation's history, where it becomes merely another add-on to a spectre of histories which have been excluded from nationalist histories. As such it needs not necessarily lead to a questioning of the dominant settlement narrative, but can instead help to perpetuate that historical narrative now that it is seen to no longer exclude other 'lesser narrative strands'. These reservations are important to keep in mind when turning to examine two of the most popular areas for anthropological fieldwork, both of which I wish to look at from the perspective of how they write themselves into the larger cultural political framework of the nation, inside which Australian anthropology continues to operate.

Two Sites of Aboriginal-Asian Cultural Exchange

There have been two major Aboriginal-Asian contact zones historically. Arnhem Land and the islands immediately north of the Northern Territory (and to a lesser extent the Kimberley coast) is one zone, the Torres Strait Islands is the other.

The most wide-ranging contribution to the discourse on the now established history of cultural exchange between Macassans and Arnhem Land Aborigines is that of C.C. Macknight. Macknight's earlier work draws attention to the neglected place granted to Aboriginal-Macassan contact history in historical work on colonial and pre-colonial Australia, when he states that 'in contrast to the relative slight interest of historians...a number of anthropologists have considered the foreign influence so readily apparent in the culture of various Aboriginal societies'.[108] Whether this shortcoming is due to the nature of historical practice or to ideological constraints is not immediately clear from this sentence. However, Macknight does point to some shortcomings in Australian historiography, which it seems he regards as evidence of a politically motivated lack of interest. Hence he raises two important points which both have the potential of

108. C.C. Macknight (ed.), *The Farthest Coast* (Melbourne: Melbourne University Press, 1969), p. 3.

challenging the way nationalist historiography represents the north as a regional bypass patiently awaiting the gradual expansion of the successful conquest of the bush in southern Australia:

> Children within sight of the very route that Tasman and Flinders sailed are taught that Captain Cook discovered Australia.[109]
>
> It might seem that the main themes of this history are discouraging: persistent failure to develop, sometimes even defeat and despair. From the point of view of distant governments this may be the case, but this is to neglect the variety and diversity of northern society, the richness of Aboriginal culture or the economic success of most non-European enterprises. For above all, this is a distinctive history, not a remote variation of Southern Australian history.[110]

Macknight directs his criticism at the received monothematic narrative of Australian history and its exclusive focus on colonial beginnings in the southeast. He draws attention to the neglected narratives from other parts of the continent, which tell a different story about colonial beginnings. As such his approach is aimed at shifting Australian historiography towards a perspective which emphasises the coexistence of a regionalised plethora of narratives about colonial beginnings. However, this vision rests on the assumption that supplementary narratives are not seen to challenge the monothematic narratives, but merely makes the settlement narrative more inclusive with the addition of particularist histories. In the previous Chapter, I discussed the dangers involved in the shifting consensus model and also suggested the necessity of embracing more radical critiques of the nation's narrativation. Similarly, it is possible to tease out a more radical critique of Australian national historiography's obsession with narrating the story of successful colonisation of the continent, by drawing attention to Macknight's same desire to include the neglected North in a more 'truly' national narrative of colonial beginnings. Despite

109. *The Farthest Coast*, preface, p. vi.

110. *The Farthest Coast*, preface, p. vi.

its false starts, in Macknight's reading the North deserves to be included in the national progression model.

While this reading of Macknight draws attention to the circumscribed nature of his critique of received histories he does involuntarily lend himself to a far more radical perspective when he argues:

> If one ignores political boundaries and looks on the sea as a unifying rather than divisive agent, a strong case can be made for regarding the north coast of Australia as the final extremity of Southeast Asia.... This returns us to the question of the role of the Macassan in Australian history.
>
> Although they did not settle permanently, it is surely reasonable to accept men who returned to the coast again and agsain over many years as in a sense *Australians*...they were the first representatives of complex societies to visit the continent consistently and find a resource that could be sold on the markets of the world.[111] (my italics)

This acceptance of the Macassans as Australians and the identification of Australia's north with Asia certainly would find little favour with cultural historians at the time when Macknight was writing and it is debatable whether that situation has really changed.[112] It certainly puts a controversial question mark against the idea of Australia as the island continent, sufficient onto itself, uniquely isolated and hence intrinsically different from the countries closest to it.[113]

---

111. *The Farthest Coast*, p. 128.
112. This would depend on one's reading of the much spoken of 'Asian turn'.
113. The argument is vigorously upheld in both cultural and natural history debates. In relation to cultural history this book is precisely about challenging the assumption of 'natural' allegiances. In relation to natural history debates the 'Australian island' position has to draw on a different explanation, as parallels to Europe are absurd and end up with the detrimental effects of introduced European animals. Instead the 'Australian island' position often invokes the uniqueness of the Australian nature, yet as Tim Flannery has shown in *The Future Eaters* even from this perspective Australia is part of a region that encompasses New Zealand, New Guinea, and the eastern parts of the Indonesian archipelago.

When I argue that Macknight's radical intervention is involuntary, it is because there is little evidence to support a deeper vein of subversion in his writing, on the contrary. For although Macknight problematises convenient narratives of settlement in a cut-off primitive world,[114] he unfortunately also reiterates the received culture argument about the primitive state of Aboriginal culture(s). As such he creates a new naturalisation of conquest through his argument about

114. In a curious turnabout Macknight virtually reverses his position in an article, 'Outback to Outback: The Indonesian archipelago and northern Australia' published in *Indonesia: Australian Perspectives* (eds.) J.J. Fox, R.G. Garnaut, P.T. McCawley, J.A.C. Mackie (ANU, 1980, pp. 137-48), when he argues that:

> The Arafura and Timor Seas comprise one of the clearest geo-political divides in history.... Before looking at the relatively minor ways in which this boundary has been crossed, it is worth emphasizing the obviousness of the divide. (Macknight, p. 137)

Macknight's article appears in an obvious political context, which is directly connected to the issue of nationhood, and as such may represent an effort to exercise caution lest one overemphasises the importance of Indonesian-Australian connections. A reading that is supported by Macknight's concluding point:

> Despite the variety of contacts across the divide none of these contacts from the area of the divide has been of continuing significance to either side...Australian and Indonesia may be neighbours, but only their back fences adjoin and both live, for the most part at the other end of their blocks. To put the point without metaphor, it is very much easier to get from Jakarta to Sydney than from Darwin to Kupang, and that will be a continuing feature of Australia's Indonesian connection and Indonesia's Australian connection. (p. 145)

Macknight's observation is interesting for its own contradictory status, in particular because of the way it runs counter to his earlier assertion of the need to show a diversity of beginnings. In fact he would appear to express the view that an opening up of colonial beginnings is mirrored by the nation's enclosure of its territory from intrusion outside its centralised control. Hence the emphasis on contact passing through Jakarta and Canberra may do little else than draw attention to the ways in which the nation asserts its own territoriality by controlling the channels of communication. Indeed, as I pointed out earlier, it is when the Australian state asserts control over its borders that communication between Aborigines and Macassans and between Torres Strait Islanders and Papuans are cut off. Macknight in this way conveys the unproblematised gaze of the modern state upon its marginalised territories. Indeed, the nation may arguably be said to affirm its control through an effective ideological patrolling of its border zones.

the Macassans as the first traders (and representatives of a 'complex society'), the Europeans becoming an equally natural chronological second, and in this way trade equals capitalism equals modernity. Trade dictates the development of the contact history in Australia's north, the incursion of the government puts an end to it:

> The end of this industry is quite clear: after about 30 years of decline, in large part due to the Customs duties and licence fees exacted by the South Australian Government, that Government decided in 1906 to restrict the issue of licences to locally owned trepanging vessels. One last prau came in the 1906-07 season to test this restriction.[115]

Also here Macknight gives no other arguments than economic rationalism. There is no indication of how the larger colonial and neo-colonial manoeuvres on either side of the Arafura Sea are instrumental in bringing this trade and contact pattern to an end.

Initially, in his article, Macknight briefly summarises the beginning and the end of Macassan-Arnhem Land Aboriginal contact history. As such his reading stresses the episodic nature of the contact history, and more importantly in relation to how it may be read today, this history is readily contained as an experience of the past which has little bearing on present day concerns, nationally or locally. Having already presented his comparative view between Macassans and the Dutch as representatives of complex societies on the one side, and 'primitive' Aboriginal society on the other, it is hardly surprising that he equates the (unrecorded) Macassan view of the Aborigines with the (recorded) Dutch view:

> The initial impression the Macassans received of the Aborigines was probably not dissimilar from that recorded by the early Dutch explorers, that they were a race of naked savages with whom little trade was to be done.[116]

While it is not immediately clear from this sentence, why the Macassans should hold the same view as the Dutch, there

115. C.C. Macknight, 'Macassans and Aborigines', *Oceania*, Vol. XLII, no. 4, June, 1972, p. 284.

116. 'Macassans and Aborigines', p. 285.

are only two possible explanations given the larger cultural conceptual framework Macknight has erected around the contact zone. Either the Macassans have taken over the Dutch view, a reading that is based on the idea of the transfer of imperial cultural outlook onto its colonial subjects, or, as I argued above, Macknight's reading of the situation is premised on his idea that 'advanced' cultures administer the same patronising gaze on 'primitive' cultures. Either way the encounter is framed within a colonialist discourse of superior and inferior cultures, and in any case what the Macassan thought is virtually sheer speculation. Certainly, the examples Macknight cites as (later) evidence of a condescending Macassan view of local Aboriginal culture are far from unequivocal.

Indeed, Macknight himself soon begins to suggest a more nuanced view may have been held by the Macassans, even if that is due to a strategic acceptance of the Aborigines that need not be genuine respect.[117] This strategic acceptance is, in Macknight's reading due to the Macassans' indifference to colonisation through invasion of the land, which again shows that the implicit but unvoiced comparison is with the European (in this case British-Australian not Dutch) history in the same area:

> To the end, the Macassans, who sought no more of the land than the beaches on which to camp, were spared the necessity of converting their initial caution into the aggressiveness needed to take a larger possession of the land....
>
> Both sides had an interest in establishing and maintaining good relations. On the Macassan side, it was obviously more efficient, and therefore profitable, if the collection and preservation of the trepang could proceed unhindered by the threat or the reality of attack. In addition there was some slight trade to be done.[118]

Ultimately, in Macknight's reading relations are governed by Macassan economic rationalism and Aboriginal self-interest,

117. See 'Macassans and Aborigines', pp. 285-86 and 290.

118. 'Macassans and Aborigines', pp. 285-86.

both of which overwhelmingly favour friendly relations. This represents a very different account from that of early European encounters in Australia's southeast which in conventional Australian histories have been narrated predominantly either as (unstrategic) misunderstandings or the inevitable dispossession of Aborigines due to European settlement (as opposed to trading posts). Both positions are rather naive readings of the operations of empires in the European expansionist phase and premised on a clear separation between interested and disinterested European pursuits.

Macknight's reading of the contact history in the north is informed by the history of European colonialism elsewhere, that is, the explanatory framework is conditioned by a view of contact history that is inseparable from colonialism. This is evident when Macknight explains the nature of the contact between Aborigines and Macassans:

> Essentially, the picture is that of two cultures existing side by side, involved neither in major co-operation nor in competition. This is not to say that both sides were not affected by the contact, but that the activities of both the Macassans and the Aborigines could have been, and often were, carried on in the absence of the others with little or no difference.[119]

What Macknight paints here is a familiar dualistic picture of the peaceful/hostile coexistence of two cultures, however, it is also one that is premised on a particular reading of cultural contact zones, which suggests that dynamic cultural exchange is not possible without a struggle for domination. Cultural encounters of significance are in this reading strategic moments of competition and as such it would seem inevitably connected to some form of colonialism. Yet, it is important to remember that the frame Macknight has established for discussing the cultural exchange, operates within a Western paradigm. This happens to such an extent that unquestioned parallels can be drawn between European and Macassan attitudes. Additionally, if parallels were to be drawn between a Macassan and a Dutch (and really also a British-Australian) reading

119. 'Macassans and Aborigines', p. 290.

of Aboriginal culture, one would have thought that the simultaneous European colonialism in Australia and in the Indonesian archipelago would have constituted an obvious framework for such an excavation. It lies beyond the scope of this book to explore further the colonial situation on the Indonesian side, but I do wish to raise a few points which contextualise some of the concerns about the problems involved in carrying out an anthropological/archaeological exploration on the Aboriginal side and juxtaposing this with a detached reading of the Macassan presence in Australian waters.

First of all the Macassans were originally not fishermen/traders but farmers and their newfound status was produced by the effects of two waves of colonialism, first a Muslim period which led to the expansion of trade in the area, and then a subsequent colonisation by the Portuguese and (later on) the Dutch. The Bugis and Makassar rulers entered into joint ventures with Malay traders.[120] Makassar then developed into a multicultural environment through the arrival of the 'Malay community, which had moved there from Siang around 1550, and the Portuguese community, which began to settle there after 1580'.[121] Makassar becomes Muslim by the 1600s and an important market 'with prices sometimes cheaper than in the Moluccas themselves'[122] 'The Malay community contributed a great deal to these developments. Their fleet, together with the Bandanese and Javanese, dominated the spice trade to and from Makassar.'[123] It is the Javanese struggle with the Dutch which opens the way for a Makassar fleet and the Bugis participation in local trade. The Dutch arrive, they win a war and insist on a monopoly on trade:

> This obliged Makassar to dismantle most of its fortifications, give up any trade in spices, stop importing foreign goods from any source other than the Dutch East India Company, expel the Portuguese and renounce

120. Christian Pelras, *The Bugis* (London: Blackwell, 1996), p. 120.

121. Pelras, p. 132

122. Pelras, p. 139.

123. Pelras, p. 139.

> any kind of suzerainty either over other parts of the archipelago or over Bugis lands.[124]

In the end it is then the Dutch colonisation that produces the instrumental changes in local trade patterns that leads to the beginning of the trepang fishery along the North Australian coast. This is also consistent with the date generally agreed upon for the beginning of the trepang fishery, somewhere in the early 18th century. The paradoxical point then is that in interesting ways the contact between Macassans and Aborigines challenges the perceived ideas of Australia as an untouched, isolated continent until the arrival of the Europeans. Macassan trade predates European colonisation history in Australia, which leads anthropologists to look at it as an instance of non-European contact between two cultures. Yet the Macassans have for centuries been involved in cross-cultural contacts at home in what comes across as a multiethnic community, and have been influenced by European contact as well as colonisation by the Dutch (and Muslims). So the non-European contact is in important ways informed by colonialism, as is its closure. Dutch colonial authorities bring to a halt the Macassan trepang fishing off the Australian coast, at the same time as the South Australian authorities decide to grant licences only to 'local' fishermen.

One last aspect needs to be considered in Macknight's interpretation of Macassan-Aboriginal encounters, which will connect the Arnhem Land Aboriginal-Asian contact discussion to the Torres Strait Islander — Papua contact history and its interpretation in anthropological representations. The obsession with contact and border zones in the anthropological debates on Aborigines and Macassans betrays the importance of contact zones to how anthropologists structure their arguments. It becomes a particularly charged situation in the Australian context, because the Aboriginal contacts were with people outside Australia itself, so behind the anthropological concerns the nation looms large. It is also for this reason that the nature of the contact, and how that influences cultural change, leads to the most charged arguments in the anthropological discourse on Aboriginal non-European contact

124. Pelras, p. 143.

history. Particularly in the attention dedicated to the contact between Aborigines and Macassans, although interestingly the contact history between Torres Strait Islanders and Papuans is much longer and far more interwoven. It is hard not to see this as a consequence of anthropological models of diffusion, where knowledge, technological innovation is supposed to trickle down from the more advanced to the lesser advanced culture. It is indirectly the unease overtaking this model too far, which drives Macknight's view on diffusion in its Arnhem Land context:

> One major difficulty with virtually all this previous work by Australian ethnographers has been the failure to look for the models which the Aborigines are supposed to have imitated. In fact, it would sometimes appear as if any unusual element in Aboriginal culture has been attributed to "Malay influence". Any claims to specifically Macassan influence should indicate the precise element in Macassarese-Buginese culture which has produced the effect, and also the presence of the Macassans in the relevant area or the line of connection to such an area. Enough is now known about the Macassans to set some limit to their usefulness as a general ragbag source of the unusual.[125]

Macknight also points out that 'even a discussion of indirect influence should attempt to show the specific or general stimuli which initiated the process'.[126] Yet if Macknight draws attention to the problem of identifying any change or difference within local Aboriginal cultures with Macassan influence, he has little to say about change within a culture, and the implicitly static view of Aboriginal culture that stems from seeking to identify change with outside influence. Instead Macknight proceeds to look at different areas in which contact and influence might be detected, and to determine the validity of any such claims on the basis of empirical evidence. In the end Macknight at some length concludes on the nature and extent of Macassan influence on Aboriginal culture:

---

125. 'Macassans and Aborigines', p. 291.

126. 'Macassans and Aborigines', p. 291.

> From the above list, it is evident that Macassan influence has been quite extensive in certain aspects of Aboriginal life, but that it did not transform the fundamental bases of society. Furthermore, this influence was only felt directly in the areas immediately contiguous to the region of contact.... There is no certain evidence of influence beyond the normal limits of travel by an Aborigine who might have met the Macassan himself, except possibly for the disposal of a few iron implements. The geographical spread of various elements of Macassan influence is a question deserving further study, but it is outside the scope of the present work.
>
> There are a number of reasons why the contact did not produce an even greater effect on Aboriginal culture and society. The most obvious is the seasonal and fairly transitory nature of Macassan activity in Australia. In addition, only a very limited part of the total Macassarese-Buginese culture was exhibited in the course of a voyage and only the relatively small number of Aborigines returning to Macassar saw anything of agriculture, permanent buildings and the full range of social and religious life. Few Macassan items, even of material culture, fitted easily into the pattern of Aboriginal life.[127]

Some of Macknight's conclusions are premised on the lack of documentary evidence that would directly link Aboriginal cultural practices further inland with Macassan influence. Based on empirical observation this obviously is the only conclusion that can be reached, yet it seems highly unlikely that during such a sustained contact period, which even includes trips made by Aborigines to Sulawesi, the cultural influence should not have travelled beyond the immediate contact zone. There is plenty of evidence showing extensive trade and cultural exchange between Aboriginal groups, and it seems somewhat incredible that the prolonged and radical exchange between Aborigines and Macassans would not feature in intertribal communication. This brings us back to the material culture view, which has haunted anthropological practice, and which associates 'primitive culture' too rigidly with physical

127. 'Macassans and Aborigines', p. 316.

observable change in instances such as Aboriginal cultural practice. This is not to argue that a new departure would uncover large chunks of material, and open up a different view of an Aboriginal culture profoundly changed by Macassan contact, for regardless of whether this was the case or not, the evidence available is too fragmented to allow such far-reaching conclusions. However, it is important to stress that there is a danger in relying too heavily on physical evidence only, both because of the lack of reliable historical evidence, and the interest which the existing evidence might have served. Hence colonialism's obsession with recording its own impact on indigenous culture tends to lead to the dismissal of other competing contact histories, also because it serves to strengthen colonialism's legitimisation of its imposed monopoly. Unfortunately, Macknight indirectly lends support not only to the colonialist narration of imminent domination, but also of colonialism's legitimation of its own practice through its axiom of inevitable competition and struggle for hegemony between two cultures in a contact zone:

> However, the underlying cause for the limitations to the influence was that there was no pressing economic or ideological competition between the two cultures. In comparison, the deep effects on Aboriginal culture and society induced by European contact in this area have usually been produced by far fewer European individuals and over a much shorter period, but these few have made insistent demands for land and sometimes for labour, together with usually well-meaning attempts to introduce "proper" notions of dress, social custom and religion.[128]

In this fashion Macknight has created a no-win situation for cultural encounters. Either inter-cultural engagement will unavoidably lead to a struggle for domination, or if coexistencc continues it means contact was too insignificant to lead to competition. The conclusion Macknight draws on what he sees as the circumscribed nature of Macassan intervention in Aboriginal society is definitive:

---

128. 'Macassans and Aborigines', p. 316.

> This is not to imply that without European intervention, the Macassans would eventually have brought about a revolution in the fundamental bases of Aboriginal life...bearing in mind the dreary saga of European attempts to promote agriculture in northern Australia, the expectation by White that the Aborigines would adopt from the Macassans a revolution as fundamental as agriculture seems naive. Rather, Macassan influence contributed merely an exotic colour to the cultural fabric of certain Aboriginal societies. While this colour might have become more marked had the contact been more prolonged, the underlying pattern was still very clear, even in areas of strongest influence.[129]

Macknight's dismissal of the Macassans' potential as introducers of agriculture into Aboriginal society is definitive, but rests on implicit notions of what constitutes cultural change. Why should Aborigines in Arnhem Land adopt farming methods? Would changes in Aboriginal social practice, trade patterns etc. not constitute such a fundamental change? What informs Macknight's reading is a diffusion model through which an evolutionary pattern can be traced back through the various cultures to the four stages, which Adam Smith described as the four significant stages of development. As has since been pointed out in the critique of the Enlightenment's blindness towards its own self-glorification (Smith's most developed state interestingly enough is commerce, which conveniently locates Britain at the apex of development), such a development hinges on a European model that again is dependent on climate, domestic animals and a whole host of other conditions, that were simply not there in Australia (and many other places). Why should other cultures' ways of doing things necessarily be transmitted or adapted? The important point about the impact of colonialism is precisely that it is not governed by choice or adaptation, but an imposition followed by an adaptation that is inscribed by colonialism.

The importance of understanding colonialism's significance for how European-indigenous contact zones have operated

129. 'Macassans and Aborigines', pp. 317-18.

in Australian colonial history has grown to the extent that anthropologists have begun to see this issue as instrumental in determining relations between the two sides. I wish to finish this Chapter by looking at how such a 'colonial anthropology' may merit some more satisfactory clues as to cultural encounters between Europeans and indigenous Australian peoples, as well as to further a deeper understanding of the contact between indigenous Australians and 'Asians' in another historical contact zone, The Torres Strait.

Torres Strait Island Contact History

In contrast to the contact zone between Aborigines and Macassans, the contact history between Torres Strait Islanders and Papuans was not produced by changes brought on by colonialism, but has a much longer and far more extensive history as John Mulvaney and Johan Kamminga argue in their *Prehistory of Australia*:

> For some 250 years Indonesians (Macassans) have visited Arnhem Land to collect trepang and, although direct influence on local cultures is demonstrable, there is no definitive evidence of more widespread consequences. For a far longer period there existed sustained transfer of culture across Torres Strait, between coastal people in southern Papua and the Aborigines of Cape York... Long-distance trading expeditions in Torres Strait, which facilitated two-way cultural diffusion between Papua and Australia's northeast, may have begun millennia ago, but the evidence for island occupation is limited to the last few hundred years. Enduring cultural influences on New Guinea transmitted by Asian seafarers began during the expansion of Austronesian-speaking people expansion eastwards across the Pacific thousands of years ago. Some of these acquired cultural traits may have been taken across Torres Strait and ultimately incorporated into Australian culture.[130]

Other anthropologists have tended to see the Torres Strait more in terms of an absolute divide than as a cultural contact zone. Hence Macknight appears almost conspicuously eager

130. *Prehistory of Australia*, p. 261.

to dismiss the significance of any pre-colonial traffic between indigenous Australians and their northern neighbours, also in the Torres Strait:

> The Arafura and Timor Seas comprise one of the clearest geo-political divides in history.... This division is not so sharp at its eastern extremity in Torres Strait, yet even here the distribution between New Guinea and Australia remains a real one.[131]

Macknight refers to the work of one particular anthropologist, D. Walker and his book, *Bridge and Barrier: The Natural and Cultural History of The Torres Strait,* to support the claim about the Torres Strait divide. Ian McNiven sums up the positions held by anthropologists on the Torres Strait as a contact zone:

> Torres Strait has long held a special place in anthropology and archaeology due to its strategic position between the Australian and Papua New Guinean mainlands and A.C. Haddon's 1898 Cambridge Anthropological Expedition. For the most part, research interests have been directed towards documenting the selective diffusion of so-called higher cultural traits of 'advanced' Papuans to their 'primitive' Aboriginal neighbours across the Torresian divide (e.g. McCarthy 1940, 1970, see also Smith 1930, 1933). These views gave rise to the concept of Torres Strait as a 'cultural filter' for, or 'cultural barrier' to, material cultural traits.[132] (Walker 1972)

It is interesting to note that what constitutes the interest in Torres Strait Islanders is not the islanders themselves, but their location at a border zone that is granted significance through the existence of the modern nation's borders, and because of a former anthropological expedition to the area. The occlusion of other readings outside this frame, invites a perusal of the motives governing anthropological practice in the area, as well as a questioning of the anthropological models

---

131. Macknight, 'Outback to Outback', pp. 137-38.

132. Ian J. McNiven, 'Enmity and Amity: Reconsidering Stone-headed Club (*gabagaba*) Procurement and Trade in Torres Strait', *Oceania*, vol. 69, pp. 94-115, p. 94.

applied. Hence the opposites of 'cultural filter' and 'cultural barrier' is a product of the diffusion model itself, and is an excellent example of anthropological models tendency to frame arguments into deterministic representations.

Two other contemporary anthropologists, Maureen Fuary and Jeremy Beckett, have come up with different answers which aren't premised on isolating the exchange of technologies and cultural practices between two already formed and as such discrete cultures, and have instead focused on the Torres Strait contact zone itself. To both the very fact of the contact zone's existence generates their explanations of what drives the Torres Strait communities, that is, it is the fact of the contact zone which drives the dynamic of both cultures. Indeed, this leads inevitably to an emphasis on *culture as process* instead of as *discrete entities.* Maureen Fuary identifies the importance of the contact with Papuans for the Torres Strait Islanders in the following way:

> Traditionally the Kulkalgal of Tudu-Yam occupied an intermediary position in the Torres Strait, both geographically and culturally, and played a significant role in inter-island and island-Papuan exchange networks. They commanded fishing, shell-fishing and travel along the extensive Warrior Reefs (Haddon 1935: 75), and maintained their power base through the advantages of trade and involvement in endemic warring and the taking of heads.
>
> Because of its central location, peoples from the Eastern and Western islands in the Torres Strait travelled to Tutu to trade. Beckett (1978) and Moresby (1876) attributed the power of the Kulkalgal to this prime location, and to their ownership of several large canoes originating in *Dawdhay* (Papua). Exchange networks criss-crossed the area, connecting Torres Strait Island peoples with each other, with Cape York peoples to the south, and with coastal Papuans to the north. So critical was the connection with Papua, that Beckett has claimed the regional Torres Strait economy was 'underwritten' by the Papuans.[133] (1987: 26)

---

133. Maureen Fuary, 'Torres Strait and *Dawdhay*: Dimensions of Self and Otherness on Yam Island', in *Oceania*, vol. 70, pp. 219-30, p. 221.

The pursuit of such different readings naturally owes much to the interpretation of quite often inconclusive evidence. Behind the choice of interpretation lurks the far more unsettling and far-reaching question of the approach taken by the anthropologist, and as I have suggested earlier, the anthropologist's own situatedness. This is a path that even critical anthropologists are exceedingly shy of following. Hence, to give just one localised example, though Nicholas Thomas in *Possessions* draws attention to the way in which a colonialist legacy continues to inform 'white settler' readings of indigenous art, there is no critique raised at the complicit part that has been played by anthropologists in the process of assessing indigenous art (as well as in other areas such as settling land claims).[134] Nor is there any hint that this may continue to haunt contemporary anthropological practice. The point is not the need to draw attention to anthropology's earlier instrumentality in asserting control over the indigenes, but to ask whether deeply questionable ideas about cultural hierarchies, might still be informing anthropological thinking. Certainly, the survival of the diffusion model would seem to indicate so. Furthermore, it is difficult to see how a reformulation of anthropological practice can succeed without foregrounding the limitations of former practices, and incorporating such an awareness into one's renewed practice. If it is generally accepted that at least some anthropologists in the past were governed by the best of intentions, yet perpetuated ideas derived from Euro-centric cultural hierarchies, what is it in contemporary anthropological thinking that guarantees its transformation of or freedom from such thinking?

Maureen Fuary's article represents a step in the direction of acknowledging colonial history's formative contribution to the anthropological field. Hence she opens her article with a quotation that draws attention to the narrative intrusion of

134. Howard Morphy in *Ancestral Connections* writes in a similar vein to Thomas when he cautions against excluding colonial history as well as its legacy (see p. 3), unfortunately without developing an argument about how either may influence anthropological practice other than drawing attention to the impact of colonial history.

Papuans into Torres Strait Islander oral history, a process to which colonialism contributes in paradoxical ways:

> The transformation of Yam Island people from a majority group through the processes of colonialism...has provided the context and impetus for the development and maintenance of their contemporary expressions of cultural identity...the past and present operate as overlapping domains along a continuum: there is an absence of sharp and clear-cut discontinuities between one era and another. For instance the pre-colonial, pre-Christian past locally referred to as *bipo taym* cannot be absolutely differentiated from the beginning of the Christian era: what is often imagined as a dichotomy is in essence a blurred boundary.... It is this tracking between the past and the present, and between Yam Island, the rest of Torres Strait and the Papuan mainland, which provides Yam Island people with the dynamic of their identity.[135] (Fuary 1991; 1993)

If Fuary addresses the issue of cultural exchange she also considers the importance of political territoriality. What is seen here is a people defined through the workings of cultural processes which are informed and in certain ways determined by colonialism. What is even more interesting in relation to the idea of establishing a different kind of anthropological practice, however, is the overt way in which Fuary draws attention to her own approach, which is defined through her interest in the nation's intrusion into a remote corner of its territory:

> I draw upon some examples from Yam, a small island community in the Torres Strait, anchored firmly within the borders of Australia, to show that with the emergence of Papua New Guinea as an independent state, an extra dimension or layer has been added to the ways in which they have come to perceive themselves and their Papuan neighbours.[136]

135. Fuary, p. 227.

136. Fuary, p. 219.

Fuary's approach is governed by an interest in an archaeological investigation into the nature, extent and length of the contact history, as well as an exploration of how that history relates to the territoriality of the nation and its demands and influences on the indigenous population. Hence her article can productively be separated into sections under the headings of; the contemporary nation and its control over its indigenous subject; colonialism (trade, military presence and missionary activities), and a post-colonial phase where the indigene operates simultaneously as an agent of the state controlling its vulnerable border zones and as a suppressed subject. The post-colonial here redefines the positions held by the different groups during colonialism, while drawing attention to the continuity of their unequal positions. I will briefly recapture these processes in the following and then turn specifically to ask what new light this throws on the idea of cross-cultural contact, and what new departures are offered for better understanding the dynamics of cultural processes.

The most important difference between Fuary's approach and that of previous anthropologists in the region is the central space granted to colonialism and its effect on existing contact patterns on the island of Yam, Fuary's site for her research:

> Dramatic changes for Torres Strait Island people were heralded with the intermittent appearance of Europeans in their waters from the 1600s, and their more regular incursions in the 1840s. During the first few decades of sustained contact with outsiders, traditional power bases were fundamentally altered. Commercial fisheries in concert with missionary and government activity in the Torres Strait region since the late 1800s effected innumerable changes in the islands. Through the bêche-de-mer and pearl shelling industries alone, warfare was discouraged, Yam-Tudu social organisation was undermined, and the micro-environments of their tiny islands were badly damaged. They became increasingly sedentary and progressively men, women and children were forced to work schedules which not only interrupted their traditional schedules, but meant they now worked for a master. On Tudu there was an uneasy balance

> of truce and warfare between the Kulkalgal and the invaders.[137]

The major shift that occurs in the colonial phase represents for the islander an altered state from individual to colonial subject. Colonialism is an onslaught that brings state, religious and military pressure to bear on the islanders. The nexus between colonialism and missionary activities represents a particularly destructive force:

> By the time the London Missionary Society missionaries approached the Central Islands of the Torres Strait in the 1870s, the Kulkalgal had already been brought under a good deal of control by the use of colonial and individual force on the frontier. The missionaries were involved in banning particular cultural practices, the destruction of sites of significance, regulation of social life, the introduction of new material goods, training clergy, creating new positions of leadership and influence, and introducing new ideas and new rituals, both secular and sacred.[138] (Fuary 1991)

In Fuary's reading there is little evidence of an emerging post-colonial world until in very recent times. The continued repression of Aborigines and Torres Strait Islanders generally after Federation is a familiar story that need not be recapitulated here. However, it is important to remember that Aboriginal and Torres Strait Islander colonialism continues and becomes in certain ways strengthened after Federation, when the independent Australian nation asserts its territorial control over the border zones in the Arafura Sea and the Torres Strait. When the reserves are finally abolished in the Torres Strait (in the 1980s) leading to a nominal 'post-colonial autonomous state', the legacy of colonial self-identity continues to coexist with a self-proclaimed identity as simultaneously Torres Strait Islander and paradoxically, Australian. This situation creates what Fuary describes as 'contradictions of self and community':[139]

137. Fuary, p. 221.

138. Fuary, pp. 221-22.

139. Fuary, p. 222.

> Central to this Yam Island sense of self is a recognition of the long term processes of colonialism by which they acknowledge and celebrate their descent from a number of peoples: the fierce Tudu men and women; a variety of Pacific Islander, South East Asian and Caribbean men and women; women and men from other Torres Strait Islands; and from specific Papuan villages.... The environment serves as a physical and social metaphor of belonging, association, and tradition: it constitutes a vehicle for symbolically expressing an historical and cultural identity unique to Yam people.[140]

The Torres Strait Islander identity is in Fuary's reading determined not by the expected embrace of a separate, indigenous identity, that is, an ontological identity constituted by a unique separateness that has somehow survived the prolonged colonial intrusive phase, but precisely through the process of working through the islanders' colonial predicament. This becomes then the acceptance of a hybrid identity, both in terms of self-identification and through the recognition of one's identity in the wider community, where the boundary is defined by a geo-environmental zone.

One of the consequences of the intrusion in colonial times and later neo-colonial interventions by the Australian government is the disruption of the established patterns of identification as Yam Islanders in one situation (or by one set of people) and Papuan in another (or by another set of people):

> Of those extended families who steadfastly identify as Yam Island people, most contain at least one member who has a Papuan parent, grandparent or great-grandparent, a Papuan spouse, or a child to a Papuan. These families do not consider themselves Papuan; in fact, they regularly downplay these genealogical ties. In terms of self-definition they are Yam Island people, but they may be externally defined by others, particularly bureaucrats or short-term visitors, as Papuan.[141]

---

140. Fuary, p. 222.
141. Fuary, p. 223.

It is interesting here how the bureaucracy of the modern Australian state continues the practices of identification of 'self' and 'other' into categorical entities, where the fact of belonging to several categories at the same time is regarded as a transgression of the rules of division. In this way the bureaucratic assertion of one place/culture of belonging represents the state's assertion of its territorial rights over the Torres Strait Islanders through the exclusion of Papuans. This amounts in effect to the state's denial of the contact history through the substitution of a new history of territorial integrity. Fuary draws attention to the problems created by the state's insistence on defining centrally the flow in and out of its territories. The state's patrolling of its border zones is increasingly obsessive, because the border zones due to a combination of their blurred state and remoteness, present a threat to an absolute cross-border control:

> Trading relations between Yam Islanders and their Papuan neighbours continue to be maintained, celebrated and staunchly defended. Canoes and dinghies from Mabaduan, and to a lesser extent Tureture, regularly visit Yam Island. In the 1980s when quarantine regulations were introduced prohibiting the movement of foodstuffs between Papua and the islands, Yam Islanders stressed that the esteemed bush foods of taro, yams and bananas had always been crucially important exchange items, and had sustained them for generations.[142]

Ironically and paradoxically the simultaneous identification as indigenous sovereign citizen and colonial subject (dependence on welfare, suffering dietary problems and so forth) opens other avenues of opportunity to Torres Strait Islanders as agents of the state:

> Given that in early to mid 1999 there were several incidents of people being smuggled into various places in Far North Qld, NSW and WA, the political significance of Torres Strait Islanders continuing to perform a *de facto* role of being the 'eyes and ears' of government...cannot be under-estimated. For in the Torres

142. Fuary, p. 223.

> Strait it is they who keep at bay 'the Other' in all its manifestations.[143]

The Torres Strait Islanders' situation in a border zone with a long history of cross-cultural interaction places them in an uncertain position, because their self-identification and conceptualisation of place sits so ill with the Australian federal state's assertion of their status as citizens of Australia. The Australian state's insistence on alienating relations between Torres Strait Islanders and Papuans leads to an internal split in the individual islander, because the definition granted by the state runs counter to traditional patterns of identification, at the same time as it lures the islander with the promise of recognition as Australian citizens through their participation in upholding the border. This coercive move by the state is an important instrumental manoeuvre in its desire for making the border absolute and strengthening its hold on the nation's blurry edges:

> Many Yam islanders express an ambivalence toward PNG. While their tiny island is in many ways regarded as something of a Papuan 'outpost', Yam Island people are trying to come to grips with their 'Papuan-ness' in relation to their 'Torres Strait Islander-ness'. On the one hand they recognise that as a people they have always relied on certain Papuan families from particular villages to constitute themselves. Their society was created by Papuans and they continue to rely and desire goods and services from Papua. This sets them apart from other Australians and paradoxically gives them their specific identity. On the other hand, there is a desire to distance themselves as Torres Strait Islanders and as Australians from their Papuan connections; to constitute themselves firmly as Torres Strait Islanders as opposed to Islanders connected to Papua. In this context a strong emphasis is placed on the 'Torres Strait Islander-ness' and therefore 'Australian-ness' and 'Queenslander-ness' of Islanders, and a de-emphasis on their 'Papuan-ness'. According to their legal status they are firmly Australians as opposed to Torres Strait Islanders with a Papuan base.[144]

143. Fuary, p. 225.
144. Fuary, p. 228.

Fuary in her explanation puts the decisive emphasis on self-identification and communal identity, and shows how this may be suppressed through colonial and neo-colonial pressures, through alienation from traditional cultural connections. I have no argument with this approach, but in order to understand how these pressures are produced it is necessary again to return to the function of the state and in particular its articulation as a modern nation. Benedict Anderson has drawn attention to how the modern formally decolonised nation has continued the colonial practice of registering its citizen, through the legacy of a colonial bureaucracy based on racially conceived difference. He singles out how in the colonial state any person can only belong to one particular category, that is, the colonial state defines and circumscribes each individual subject, and the modern nation continues this practice. Furthermore, such a classification continues to be used to single out particular groups as unwanted aliens. These groups are produced as subjects on the fringes of society, whose allegiance to the state is always regarded with suspicion. This can be read as a deliberate mechanism for preserving the dominance of particular groups by granting themselves a privileged space at the centre of definitions of both national and 'modern' characteristics, through the deliberate marginalisation of those considered most removed from, or most threatening to, such an identification. In this way the other is marginalised both temporally (labelled as culturally unadapted and often unadaptable) and spatially (on the edge of the imagined community). I have argued previously that the marginalisation, alienation, or externalised/internalised othering covers up an unease at the centre over the periphery's demonstrable otherness. In terms of the white Australia policy race and colonial history in relation to Aborigines this has also already been established.

The Mabo-case can be read as an exercise in drawing attention to the process of internal/external othering which has been central to both colonial and independent Australia. For the Aborigines and Torres Strait Islanders Mabo represents the long-awaited reopening of the files of history, whereas it is seen by the Australian state, and constructed by large sections of the influential segments of Australian society as threatening to the nation's integrity. Mabo reveals the blurry nature of the nation's claim to the continent (other than through sheer physical and economic brute force), but it is also plain to see that Mabo has shown not to be threatening to the 'white' hold on the Australian continent. Furthermore, it is an established fact that although applicable to the mainland as well as the Torres Strait, Mabo still redresses the land rights issue for only a very small minority of Aboriginal groups. What I find more interesting to pursue in this context, however, is the limitation of Mabo precisely in the border zones that I have been discussing in this Chapter. For Mabo actually delivers the definitive territorial boundaries of the Australian state, and although it grants land rights to the Torres Strait Islands in question, it fails to recognise and in important ways even undermines the cross-strait contact culture, and as such operates in the Torres Strait as another territorial encroachment of the state on its neo-colonial subject. As such, the Mabo-case serves up the nation's right to define its entire territory, in terms of (albeit a criticised) settlement history. The Mabo-case then becomes a question of whether the settlers have settled on already settled territory or not, which the verdict affirmed. As such instead of terra nullius, Australia was an already settled entity when the Europeans arrived, which can be seen in the many ethnographic maps produced of Aboriginal Australia which show a continent divided into linguistically defined indigenous groups. However, the interests of Aborigines and Torres Strait Islanders are not necessarily best served by having the discourse of territorial property confined to the boundaries of the nation state, also because this discourse indirectly legitimates that nation's absolute borders around the Australian continent, and as such incorporates the indigenes into the nation state. If these closing remarks seem an unduly harsh criticism of the intentions of the Australian state let someone else have the final words:

> Qld was permitted to acquire the islands of the Torres Strait, and this was validly executed. "She could not get New Guinea", said Sir Samuel Griffith later, "but managed to get as near as possible. We followed round as close as we could get between the islands, and the coast of New

Guinea, taking in practically everything".... As things now stand, the cumulative effect of Australian legislation is to preclude Papua New Guinea from enjoyment of substantial resources of the TS. Other than the initial acquisition of the islands by Qld, Australia has brought this about while exercising governmental control over the Territory of Papua and the Trust Territory of New Guinea. As Van der Veur, in one of his studies, concluded: "A close look at these boundaries reveals inequities, idiosyncracies, and inaccuracies".[145]

REFERENCES

Art from the Land: Dialogues with the Kluge-Ruhe Collection of Australian Aboriginal Art, ed. by Howard Morphy and Margo Smith Boles (Charlotteville: Uni. of Virginia, 1991).

Australian Perceptions of Asia. Special Issue of Australian Cultural History, no. 9, 1990, ed. by David Walker, Julian Horne and Adrian Vickers.

Barnes, Kathy, *Kiripapurajuwi Skills of Our Hands: Good Craftsmen and Tiwi Art* (Kathy Barnes, 1999).

Beckett, Jeremy, 'Aboriginal Histories, Aboriginal Myths: An Introduction', *Oceania*, vol. 65, no. 2.

Beckett, Jeremy, 'A Historical Perspective: Torres Strait Islanders and the Sea,' in M. Mulrennan, N. Hansen and the Island Coordinating Council, *Marine Strategy for Torres Strait: Policy Directions* (Darwin: ANU North Australian Research Unit and the Torres Strait Island Coordinating Council.

Berndt, R.M., 'Badu, Islands of the Spirits' *Oceania*, Vol. 19, 1948, pp. 93-103.

Berndt, R.M., 'External Influences on the Aboriginal', *Hemisphere*, Vol. 9, no. 3, 1965, pp. 2-9.

Berndt, R.M. and C.H. Berndt, *Arnhem Land: Its History and Its People* (Melbourne: Cheshire, 1954).

Boigu: Our History and Culture (Aboriginal Studies Press, Canberra, 1991).

Bonyhady, Tim and Tom Griffiths (eds.), *Prehistory to Politics: John Mulvaney, the Humanities and the Public Intellectual* (Melbourne: Melbourne UP, 1996).

Cense, A.A., 'Makassaars-Boeginese Prauwaart op Noord-Australië', *Bidragen tot de Taal-, Land- en Volkenkunde uitgegeven door het*

---

145. W.E. Holder, 'The Queensland "border": The legal position' in *The Torres Strait Islanders*, Vol. V: 'The Border and Associated Problems', ed. by E.K. Fisk, Maree Tait, W.E. Holder and M.L. Threadgold (ANU, 1974), p. 38.

Kroninklijk Instituut voor Taal-, Land- en Volkenkunde, Del 108, 1952, pp. 248-64.

Customary Marine Tenure in Australia, ed. by Nicolas Peterson & Bruce Rigsby (Sydney: University of Sydney Press, 1998).

Donaldson, I. and T. Donaldson (eds.), *Seeing the First Australians* (Sydney: Allen & Unwin, 1985).

Earl, G., *Enterprise in Tropical Australia* (London: Madden and Malcolm, 1846).

Fuary, Maureen, 'Torres Strait and *Dawdhay*: Dimensions of Self and Otherness on Yam Island,' in *Oceania*, vol. 70, pp..219-30.

Haddon, A.C., *Reports of the Cambridge Anthropological Expedition to Torres Straits* (Cambridge: Cambridge University Press, 1935).

Hamilton, Annette, '"Fear and Desire": Aborigines, Asians and the National Imaginary', in *Australian Perceptions of Asia. Special Issue of Australian Cultural History*, no. 9, 1990, ed. by David Walker, Julian Horne and Adrian Vickers, pp. 14-35.

Hulme, Peter, *Colonial Encounters: Europe and the Native Caribbean 1492-1797* (London: Routledge, 1986).

Indonesia: Australian Perspectives (eds.) J.J. Fox, R.G. Garnaut, P.T. McCawley, J.A.C. Mackie (Canberra: ANU, 1980).

Kaye, Stuart B., *The Torres Strait* (London: Martinus Nijhoff Publishers, 1997).

Kuper, Adam, *The Invention of Primitive History* (London: Routledge, 1988).

McCarthy, F.D., 'Trade in Aboriginal Australia, and "Trade" Relations with Torres Strait, New Guinea and Malaya', *Oceania*, Vol. X, pp. 171-95.

McIntosh, *Aboriginal History* (Canberra: ANU), Vol. 21, 1997.

Macknight, C.C., 'Macassans and Aborigines', *Oceania*, Vol. XLII, no. 4, June, 1972, pp. 283-321.

Macknight, C.C., 'Outback to Outback: The Indonesian archipelago and northern Australia', in *Indonesia: Australian Perspectives* (eds.) J.J. Fox, R.G. Garnaut, P.T. McCawley, J.A.C. Mackie (Canberra: ANU, 1980), pp. 137-48.

Macknight, C.C., (ed.), *The Farthest Coast* (Melbourne: Melbourne University Press, 1969).

McNiven, Ian J., Enmity and Amity: Reconsidering Stone-headed Club (*gabagaba*) Procurement and Trade in Torres Strait, *Oceania*, Vol. 69, pp. 94-115.

MacWhite, E., 'On the Interpretation of Archaeological Evidence in Historical and Sociological Terms', *American Anthropologist*, Vol. 58, 1956, pp. 3-25.

Morphy, Howard, *Ancestral Connections Art and an Aboriginal System of Knowledge* (Chicago: Chicago University Press, 1991).

Mountford, C.P., *Records of the American-Australian Scientific Expedition to Arnhem Land*, 2 Vols., (Melbourne: Melbourne University Press, 1956).

Mulvaney, D.J., '*Bêche-de-mer*, Aborigines and Australian History', *Proceedings of the Royal Society of Victoria*, Vol. 79, pp. 449-57.

Mulvaney, John and Johan Kamminga, *Prehistory of Australia* (Sydney: Allen and Unwin, 1999).

Pelras, Christian, *The Bugis* (London: Blackwell, 1996).

Searcy, Alfred, *In Australian Tropics* (Sydney: George Robertson, 1909).

Thomson, D.F., *Economic Structure and the Ceremonial Exchange Cycle in Arnhem Land* (Melbourne: Macmillan, 1949).

The Torres Strait Islanders, Vol. V: 'The Border and Associated Problems', ed. by E.K. Fisk, Maree Tait, W.E. Holder and M.L. Threadgold (ANU, 1974).

Young, Robert, *Colonial Desire: Hybridity in Theory, Culture and Race* (London: Routledge, 1995).

3

Geographic Dislocation: From European Satellite to Asian Backwater?

well let's drop this and ask what do you think of
australia's relations with asia
again in a word
if you like
asia not like australia not like asia but has to like
asia that has
not to like australia

from 'Interview with Yu', in
Ouyang Yu, *Moon Over Melbourne*

The Chinese-Australian poet and critic, Ouyang Yu, in the quotation above ponders ironically on Australia's difficult relations with its 'Asian neighbours'. This problematic international affair is often represented as a natural consequence of Australia's belated awakening interest in its own geopolitical environment and quite often seen as an embarrassing betrayal of a former Australian provincial and insular attitude to its neighbouring countries. However, while Australia's international outlook has become centred on its immediate region, questions now focus on the nature of the political agenda nourishing this new engagement with 'Asia'. An emerging Asian agenda in Australia's international relations can be traced back to World War II when the British Empire in the 'Far East' collapsed as Japan invaded Southeast Asia, forcing Australia to look for ways of filling up the gap left by the British departure.[146]

---

146. While earlier instances of Australian assertions of its own interests, such as Prime Minister Hughes's racially motivated intervention at the Versailles conference after World War I, these instances resulted from

Historically the Australian reluctance to culturally engage with Asia corresponds to a lack of interest in Asian influences on Australian self-perceptions in relation to questions of national identity internally, but equally important also in relation to Australia's projection of itself externally. It is the latter point which represents the exploratory departure for this Chapter, and as such the point is a particular manifestation of the overall concern of this book to look for less repetitive and more challenging ways of exploring constructions of Australian identity, outside the conventional settlement narrative. The aim is twofold: to displace conventional settlement discourse and to argue that part of a necessary reassessment of Australian cultural history lies in reinterpreting Australia's external relations with Asia, to find more satisfactory answers to questions related to Australian cultural historiography's assertion of Australia's exclusively European-derived tradition.

In the post-war assessment of Australia's geopolitical context, I intend to place the discussion of Australia's external relations outside the traditionally conceived, shared community with Britain and the U.S. For if Australian cultural and political attitudes to Asia have much in common with American and British attitudes, Australia's different history and location has also given a very different and indeed unique shape to its relations with Asia, even if this may have been a reluctant and forced situation rather than opportunities eagerly seized upon. My point is that Australia has been forced to acknowledge its new geopolitical situation as part of a wider process of coming to terms with its existence on the Asian-Pacific rim. This is perhaps not a controversial statement, since many others of different political observations have made a similar point. However, this represents, in my view, more than a politics of adjustment to a new situation, where Asia simply plays a far bigger role. The fall of Australia's cultural isolation from Asia also opens a door to better understand how former processes of engagement with Asia

---

an anxiety to preserve a particular make-up of the British Empire that guaranteed Australia's status under the Imperial umbrella, not as desires to speak as a nation with an autonomous outlook.

have been rendered insignificant, because they disturbed the nation's narration as a white settlement in a geopolitical vacuum.

In an earlier Chapter on Australian historiography I argued that conventional settlement histories cover up important aspects of Australian cultural history that challenge received national histories. These readings of colonial Australian history have created a view of colonial Australia as existing exclusively as either a barbaric or isolated civilisational outpost of the British Empire. I pointed out that debates over Australian cultural history have been marred by the legacy of pioneer myths concerned with settlement in the bush, followed by national baptism at Gallipoli. These myths have not only served to produce national homogeneity, but have also actively been utilised to render all other explanations and interpretations irrelevant to a national perspective.[147] This Chapter constitutes a structural and thematic parallel exercise to the Chapter on Australian historiography in so far as it draws attention to other trajectories as productive explanations of Australian cultural history. I will argue that Australia's relations with Asia cannot merely be seen as an externalised settlement discourse, between transplanted Europeans and Asians, as this merely confirms received ideas of a cultural moat operating between Australia's north on the one side and Asia on the other side. An alternative way of thinking about Australia's external relations with Asia is to see Asia as the dark shadow that haunts Australia's obsession with

---

147. This particular use of the term 'national' represents in my view a conflation between 'national' and 'nationalist', where the nationalist perspective seeks to legitimise its own reading by pointing to the 'reality' of the Australian nation's orientation. Here, it is important to distinguish between the anxiety to reproduce the Australian nation as it ideally sees itself. This can be seen clearly in the many books dealing with an evolving Australian foreign policy forced into existence by the acute isolation felt by the fall of Singapore to the Japanese and more generally to the collapse of the British Empire. These books inevitably draw a parallel between Australia's external relations and the White Australia policy. Here, quite clearly external relations are only rhetorically governed by a discourse of natural affinity with other white nations, but at a deeper level created by the desire to ignore the geopolitical location of Australia.

identifying itself as a European nation in an Asia-Pacific region. In this interpretation Australia is forced reluctantly into a politics of engagement, rather than embracing the opportunities stemming from its geopolitical position.

Political-cultural analyses of Australia's international relations have traditionally followed what seems like a self-evident chronology. They take point of departure in the evolution of Australia's colonial ties to Britain, followed by a period of unconditional attachment to the British Empire after Australia's formal independence. World War II forces a reluctant Australia to rearrange its international priorities.[148] Although after the end of the war a dual policy of dependency on Britain and the US is pursued, Australia's international interests are increasingly aligned with the US. After the Vietnam War the American withdrawal from the Asian mainland forces Australia to 'come of age' internationally and find a new position that corresponds with its actual location, no longer merely relying on, and eagerly encouraging, the ready intervention of powerful allies.

An interesting mechanism has been operating in cultural historical explorations of what may be termed Australia's externalised Asian 'other'. This mechanism has operated externally, as multiculturalism has internally, through a curiously ahistorical approach to Australia's relations with its neighbours, as if Asia suddenly materialised, when Australia began to engage with it. In terms of the political discourse this is true in so far as the public debate on Australian-Asian relations has dominated the media and the political agenda only in recent decades. However, when looking beyond the

---

148. The following quotation from P.G. Edwards, *Prime Ministers and Diplomats: The Making of Australian Foreign Policy, 1901-1949* (Melbourne: Oxford U.P., 1983) captures the inevitability of the change, and particularly the reluctance with which it was accepted:

> In 1901 Australia was a colonial federation with no right to conduct her own foreign policy. By 1949 she had...become a fully independent actor in world politics. In June 1950 Menzies called for a 'common Empire foreign policy' on 'major matters', to be coordinated by a 'Committee on Imperial Foreign Policy'...but this was probably the last time that imperial diplomatic unity was seriously proposed by a responsible Australian leader. (p. 186)

contemporary preoccupation with Asia, it is important to keep in mind the ways in which Australian-Asian relations have been operating as a strategic neglect. One example of this is the White Australia policy, which more than anything represented an effort to ignore Australia's geopolitical location, and pretend that Australia lay where its chosen allegiances lay, somewhere in the Mid-Atlantic. However, the anxiety which has in this way governed Australia's relations with Asia, betrays the looming awareness of Asia's proximity in discourses on Australia's cultural identity. Hence, it is a misreading to equate Australian involvement with its Asian neighbours with Australia's post-war military engagement in Indonesia, Korea, Malaya, Vietnam and more recently, East Timor. Even during the colonial era when Australia's foreign policy was dictated by imperial concerns in London, 'Asia' existed as an ominous and unsettling geopolitical absence in Australia's self-definition as a nation, while looming large as an equally disturbing geographical presence, most often represented through the fears of invasion by force or stealth. David Walker, in his book *Anxious Nation,* has demonstrated a strong Australian cultural preoccupation with Asia during the colonial period and the first half of the twentieth century, although he does not as such connect this infatuation with any need to redefine Australian cultural histories of the period. Rather he describes the Asian connections as an unrecognised feature that will add to Australia's cultural identity at the time, making it more diverse and by implication richer, than is commonly acknowledged by (cultural) historians. Yet such models of limitless diversification and expansion are problematic, as I have pointed out previously, in their reluctance to draw attention to the operations of hegemonic nation narratives which are determined to monopolise received cultural histories. What is needed in order to challenge rather than merely add to the already congested margins of Australian received cultural histories is a far more critically aware cultural history that shows the interactions between this new discovered cultural territory and the production of conventional settlement histories. The self-imposed limitation in Walker's scope is interesting here, for while he draws attention to Edward Said's *Orientalism* in a passage where he talks generally of how the

West has understood and produced for itself a set of representations of the East, he does not connect this to a particular brand of Australian orientalism, nor for that matter is there any reflection concerning how Walker understands *Orientalism* in his own context. In fact Walker's inclusion of Said is gratuitous, for how can one refer to *Orientalism*, without either embracing or take up the challenge this book raises through its questioning, not only about the way the West historically has constructed and imagined the East for itself, but also in contemporary times. It is my argument here, and it is certainly inspired by Said, that Australia has not only made use of the idea of 'Asia' as a process of 'othering', but that Australia's cultural history in definitive ways has been bound by a simultaneous external and internal process of 'othering'. Internally, as I will show in the Chapter on Chinese immigration, through its White Australia policy (to which can be added a process of 'othering' of the Aborigines), externally through a long historical refusal to recognise its own geopolitical position. Australia has had its own unique brand of orientalism, which, although British derived, developed its own characteristics through colonial displacement.[149] Just as Western orientalism more generally has been changed, yet in important ways continues to recycle its own images of the 'East', Australia's brand of orientalism has been changed by the emergent new nations to its north,

149. Nicholas Brown, in his article, 'Australian Intellectuals and the Image of Asia: 1920-1960', pursues a similar argument in his discussion of Asia's operation in the Australian unconscious, when he argues that, 'white settlers in Australia have contributed their own distinctive emphases to the generic opposition between Asia as the East or the Orient, and European society as Western or Occidental. In the nineteenth century their image registered opportunities and anxieties perhaps more pressing than those informing the European convention of the Orient. A colonial rather than a metropolitan construction this image drew on influences ranging from the early schemes of entrepreneurs to fears of contamination and invasion. And, as Edward Said has argued of the European context, the Australian image was inherently reflexive — although what it reflected of colonial society was not so much the sophisticated patterns of an Orientalist discourse, operating across diverse fields from literature to strategy, but a more basic attempt to define the culture and the institutions of a new society in what was seen as an alien hemisphere.' (Brown, p. 80)

yet the representation of the Australian self as besieged by 'others' with agendas seen as threatening to Australia, continues through still new variations on the fear of the 'yellow hordes syndrome' (manifestations of this are rife in the fear of Indonesia's collapse, the 'boat refugees' and the detention centre crises).

This is not the place to excavate a different colonial political legacy, but it is the place to briefly reflect on some of the problems inherent in the more recent conventional approaches to understanding Australia's geopolitical position. For in general terms they take for granted a historically determined cultural cringe which is initially directed towards a British metropolitan centre and subsequently towards an American one, only to be finally released through 'postcolonial'[150] independence and confident self-reliance. A postcolonial state here represents little more than the unproblematised modern nation narrating a past of dependencies, in this way reassuring its citizens that they have arrived at a self-confident national identity. This model of an evolving nationhood also enables the view that it is the emergence of Australia's political independence which paves the way for a new Australian attitude to its Asian neighbours. The political agendas abroad of the Labor and Liberal governments of the 1990s are two interesting examples of two long-held different attitudes to the idea of the Australian nation's international role. In the case of the Howard government its chosen foreign policy has shown little interest in developing an independent international agenda and much preparation to pay lip-service to whatever policies have emerged from Washington. As a political platform it could be labelled 'reluctant modernity'. It is a policy that paradoxically, given Howard's devotion to the concept of the 'Aussie battler', finds little in Australian policy that is not either derived from the British, or produced to accommodate the Americans. The preceding Keating government on the other hand embraced Australia's future as an integral regional part of Asia with a readiness that could be labelled over-

150. The term 'postcolonial' here refers to a geopolitical universe, although it does entail the legacy of colonialism. Hence I deliberately use this term to qualify the term 'independence'.

enthusiastic modernity. Although this policy embraced Australia's geopolitical position it had little to offer in terms of bridging the cultural divide between Australia and its neighbours. While Keating's view is the more productive and dynamic it also betrays the inherent contradictions that follow from identifying with an unproblematised achieved independence as a nation.

The reading so far of the two Prime Ministers' agendas may appear to be a case of one appearing to look to the history and the other to the future. Yet both are in effect speaking about the future role and identity of their nation by laying claim to their own preferred reading of Australia's past. John Howard embraces the idea of Australia as a continuation of British derived, now American defined political life in the South Pacific. Paul Keating asserted that Australia's past was shaped by a series of breaks with a colonial dependency. Both accounts are happily ensconced in settlement history, and bring Australia's geopolitical situation into that frame of historical explanation. When measured against the demands placed on Australia to respond to contemporary changes in its geopolitical environment, both political narratives appear inadequate. Two interesting miscalculations might be used as examples here: Keating's ill-founded gamble on developing a personal relationship with the obviously corrupt Soeharto, and Howard's failure to realise that to return to the idea of Australia as somehow geopolitically misplaced is not only an unproductive way of dealing with regional changes, but also a policy that will merely lead to misunderstandings and an isolation, which Australia can hardly afford politically or economically.[151] The general deterioration in Australia's relations with neighbouring countries has been frequently remarked upon by political commentators. Where Keating's and Howard's rhetorical definitions of Australia's international position are easily identified as antagonistic, developments in Indonesia and particularly East Timor have paradoxically forced a convergence of policies upon Australia's response to the unfolding crises.

---

151. One could add culturally as well, but granted Howard's lack of interest in Asian culture, there is little point.

In fact postcolonial Indonesia represents a good case example to confront Australian attitudes, and arguably the most pressing and consistent example of the difficulties entailed in the continuous remodelling of Australia's relationship with its neighbours. Indonesia's population size and position immediately to the north of Australia has remained a constant concern in Australian foreign policy. It is in Indonesia that Australian fears of Asian disintegration followed by waves of refugees materialize in its most acute form. It is here that Australia most strongly has taken an attitude that is not merely the expression of the nationalist rhetoric of preferred legacies alone, and from time to time this attitude has brought Australia in opposition to its traditional allies. From Australia's involvement with the decolonisation process in Indonesia, through the Malayan war in the 1950s, the Indonesian take-over of Irian Jaya in the early 1960s, the coup in 1965, and to the Indonesian debacle in East Timor, Australia's foreign policy has operated as a kind of often unsuccessful crisis management, rather than as a confident assertion of Australia's geopolitical home in the region. In the following pages I wish to concentrate my discussion on two milestones in Australia's relationship with Indonesia. First, the role played by Australia during the final years of Indonesia's struggle for independence from the Dutch and secondly Australia's role during the Indonesian invasion and later abandoned colonisation of East Timor.

The purpose of focusing on Indonesia is not only to throw new light on Australia's relations with Asia. Rather the focus on Indonesia represents a departure for a remapping of Australia's international relations in a way that challenges historically constructed ideas about Australia's 'natural' or 'objective' political interests. Behind this choice of approach lies one of the central concerns of this book, namely a problematisation of traditional conceptions about Australia's cultural roots and interests. Rather than seeing Australia's predicament over Indonesia merely as the result of a necessary but difficult new departure in its international relations, it is necessary to look at Australia's historical connections with Indonesia in order to better understand Australia's current situational difficulties. Arguably the same kind of exploration is needed in Australian relations with other Asian nations.[152] Although this does not represent an effort to make redundant traditional configurations of Australian culture, it is meant as yet another nail in the coffin of this tradition's hegemonic hold on definitions of Australian pursuits, through an excavation of the absences, which these traditional approaches have produced.

In the chapter on Chinese-Australians I discuss how multiculturalism erroneously has been associated only with the post-1945 immigration boom, and how this shows the repressive ways in which a hegemonic, nationalist tradition seeks to either exclude or assimilate alternative histories. I argue for the productiveness of looking at the challenges such alternative histories pose to ideas of a 'natural formation' of a national identity. My approach to Australia's relations with Indonesia is thematically similar, although its historical scope is narrower. This is because my interest lies primarily with Australia's political responses to Asia, here exemplified in its relations with Indonesia, and the cultural anxiety which informs the Australian response. A historical exploration of

---

152. Indeed the process of mapping out Australia's colonial and twentieth century relations with Asia has begun, for instance through the work of Eric Rolls in his two volumes on the Chinese migrants in Australia and in David Walker's *Anxious Nation,* which deals with Australia's historical infatuation with particularly East Asia, Southeast Asia and South Asia, from 1850-1939. This volume will be followed by a second volume that will trace interrelations between Australia and Asia in the second half of the twentieth century. Other books have traced Australia's political relations with various Asian nations, such as *Pathways to Asia* and Nick Knight's *Thinking About Asia.* However, such studies seek to map out that which has either been neglected, seemed irrelevant, or too obscure, rather than connecting the process of mapping with renegotiating the territorial claims made implicitly or explicitly by the previous studies. Again the approach is premised on the idea of expanding an already existing field, rather than challenging received ideas about Australia's cultural position historically. Hence, I find it revealing that although Walker's book is a pioneering effort in so far as it maps out a new understanding of Australia's relations with Asia by tracing it through Australia's colonial history, there is no reflection as to why this has not been carried out before and what it may do to received ideas about Australia's cultural history. Instead it merely talks, and briefly at that, of Australia's 'periodic rediscovery of our proximity to Asia' (Walker, p. 1).

Australia's relations with Asia can be mapped out, and could be extended back to the colonial beginnings, e.g. through the early colony's dependency on trade and contact with particularly the Dutch East Indies, India and China, as David Walker has done.[153]

There is no relationship that more directly exposes the built-in paradoxes inherent in Australian cultural perceptions of its geographic neighbourhood than Australia's engagement with Indonesia.[154] The Australian approach is governed by an overall attitude that often fluctuates between exotic enticement and alienated repulsion.[155] While such an attitude can be said to originate in the widespread ignorance about its neighbour to the north, and more generally in Australia's traditionally

---

153. Walker writes that 'From the earliest days of the British settlement of Australia, India and the crown colony of Ceylon were a familiar part of the colonists' world'. (*Anxious Nation*, p. 13). The profound influence of colonial architecture from other parts of the Empire is another example, whereas the fact that the Anglofile Prime Minister, *par excellence*, made his fortune from selling pig-iron to the Japanese in the 1930s, is a poignant illustration of how geographical reluctance among those who took upon themselves to define Australian culture and its interests were often overtaken by geographical-political realities and the nation's as well as their own economic interests. Though evidently paradoxical, such undertakings coexisted with a deep-seated racist view of Australia's neighbours to the north.

154. I focus here on the post-war relations with Indonesia for a number of reasons. A focus on colonial Indonesia would entail an exploration of the Dutch colonial policy, as well as obscure my preoccupation with the idea of Indonesia in Australian cultural politics. Also the decolonisation of Indonesia coincides with the emergence of an independent Australian foreign policy outlook. Furthermore, this Chapter although focusing on Australia's externalised 'Asian other', may in important ways be read as a parallel to the chapter on Chinese migration, in which I seek to install a historical rather than a contemporary ahistorical reading of Australia's multicultural space.

155. I am drawing on a host of books here, which all draw attention to the production of Asia in Australian politics, in the media and in cultural production generally. Alison Broinowski's highly influential *The Yellow Lady* is now a standard starting point, and was followed in 1995 by Robin Gerster's *Hotel Asia*. More recently two collections of essays, *Alter/Asians* and *Diaspora: Negotiating Asian-Australia* have tried to explore the cross-over between Australia's internalised and externalised Asian 'others'.

phobic relations with Asia, such a reading ignores the deeper implications of Australia's relations with Indonesia. Although my reading here focuses on the period after World War II I wish to begin by making a few observations on Australia's earlier historical relations with Indonesia.

Australia's relations with Indonesia actually predate both the white settlement of Australia and the formation of Indonesia into the political colonial entity, the Dutch East Indies. Macassan fishermen from Sulawesi visited the present-day Northern Territory to collect trepang, which represented a valuable commodity throughout Southeast Asia and East Asia. After their arrival and take-over of the lucrative spice trade in the East Indies, the Dutch mapped out large chunks of the Australian coastline. They showed little commercial interest in Australia and the maps served mainly to avoid wrecking Dutch ships *en route* to Batavia on the Australian coastline. The apparent lack of commercial Dutch interest in Australia has commonly (and conveniently) been offered as the explanation (and legitimisation) of the British unchallenged claim to the continent, initially to the eastern coastline during Captain Cook's brief visit to the more fertile Australian east coast, and subsequently to the continent by early governors.

In Australian historiography colonial links between Australia and the Indonesian archipelago have tended to be of marginal concern, if not completely ignored. Yet a mapping out of historical relations between Australia and its neighbours to the north will, while not necessarily challenge conventional representations of colonial history, redirect attention from conventional 'tyranny of distance' theses. While centre-periphery theories are productive for the way in which they illustrate interdependency between colony and metropolis, they tend to ignore the ways in which colonial peripheries were interconnected. As such they inadvertently fall short of challenging an important part of the premise of the imperial history, they, if critical of imperial history at all, are questioning, that is the naturalisation of the metropolis-colony axis.

An exploration of an altered focus away from the conventionally posited umbilical cord to Britain and towards Australia's more immediate geographical neighbourhood would produce more diverse explanations of colonial beginnings in the various parts of the country. The abortive attempts to found a settlement along the coastline of the Northern Territory is an illustrative case (as I argue in the Chapter on Aboriginal-Asian contacts), as is the confident predictions by the early colonial Establishment that Australia would provide the men to sustain Britain's economic and military control over its Asian Empire. A settlement in Australia's north would serve several purposes at the same time. It would be a military post from which control over shipping in the region could be exercised. It would prevent other settlements, and with an overland connection (either by land or river/lake, both options would later prove to be illusory) it would make redundant the long arduous journey around the continent. This early interest in Australia's 'Asian potential' shows how Asia has operated as a lever for colonialist dreams of expansion, but this interest has been seen as a separate theatre outside the evolving national settlement history.

The point I am pursuing here is that prevailing nationalist representations do not allow for the intrusion of Asia into the national narrative of the Australian nation. One way this exclusivist practice manifests itself is in the relegation of histories, which engage in narratives outside the colonial-metropolitan axis, to a status as parochial and regional.[156]

156. It is possible to argue for a double axis operating within the colonial-metropolitan axis, between a metropolitan (imperial) centre, a satellite or displaced metropolitan centre in the colonial periphery and a colonial periphery which operates as a satellite within the satellite. This double axis is important, for the relegation of certain colonial experiences to sideshows compared to a national narrative, mirrors the relation between the unsuccessful transplantation of European settlement and the evolving colonial community in Australia's southeast. The success criteria for settlement, that is, the modernity of the colonial project, is matched by a shadow-world of doomed settlements, and genocide. Hence the national narrative of the imperial-colonial umbilical cord can be matched by alternative histories that betray the monolithic nature of colonial modernity. This in turn shows that the idea of an ever-expanding plethora of segment histories (of Italians in the cane fields, Chinese on the gold fields and so forth) is premised on a strategy of containment. New histories can be added as long as they are not permitted to challenge the process of legitimising the Anglo-Irish derived hold on the 'History of the Australian nation'.

The term 'regional' signals not only that focus is shifted away from the hub of Australia's settlement history in the Southeast, but also that its regional status betrays a provinciality, as a sideshow of no consequence to the national narrative. One example of this type of a regional history can be found in Eric Rolls's history book, *Sojourners,* where Rolls points out that the desire for establishing a settlement in Australia's north was to get a share of the trepang trade.[157] What is interesting here is not only Rolls's focus on a different part of Australia from that which is usually central to national narratives of colonial Australia, but also that his perspective sheds light on a different pattern of cultural interchange.[158]

Sojourners explores Australia's colonial history through an Australian-Chinese perspective. As such, *Sojourners* is not a regional history, but can be described as a particularistic history of Australia, because of its highly selective perspective. While the term particularistic history writing may initially appear to draw attention to a limitation in its historical scope, I find it far more interesting to look at its contributing potential to the questioning of received national histories. In this light its particularistic nature which places it outside the uniformity of national narratives is precisely its enabling feature. Hence Rolls's focus on Chinese-Australian relations leads him to devote far more writing space on this settlement in Australia's

---

157. For Eric Rolls's description of the trepang trade, see Eric Rolls's *Sojourners: The Epic Story of China's Centuries-old Relationship with Australia: Flowers and the Wide Sea* (St. Lucia: University of Queensland Press, 1992), pp. 13-16, and for his discussion of the abortive attempts at settlement, see pp. 254-57.

158. Nor does Rolls's assessment stand alone. In 1846 G. Earl shows in *Enterprise in Tropical Australia* (London: Madden and Malcolm, 1846) that the prospect of Asian settlement in Australia was not always considered a threat:

> A considerable number [of Aborigines] have paid one or more visits to Macassar, residing there for months together, which has familiarized them with the language and manners of the people of that country, and may probably lead to a closer intercourse, should the Macassars establish themselves upon the coast. (p. 118)

Apart from this prosaic statement there is of course a whole catalogue of immigration scheme proposals aimed at attracting cheap Asian labour in colonial Australian history. Very few of these materialised.

north, than it merits in most historical presentations. The relegation of this incident to the more obscure parts of Australian history has less to do with its importance at the time, and more with conventional Australian historiography's narrative of growing settlement, which leads to abortive attempts being treated as historical aberrations. In this way the dominant nationalist perspective in Australian historiographic representation is governed by an approach which backdates Australia's current status as 'a successful, mature nation of settlers' to a year zero of beginning. Through the narrative focus on Australia's early 'modern' history as a narrative of colonial modernity Australia's contemporary modernity is confirmed as a culmination of all that went before it.[159] Eric Rolls's account of the rise and fall of one of the settlements in Australia's north can be read as a counter narrative to the modernity-driven narrative of struggling, perhaps, but inevitably always successful settlement:

> This time they found good water and within a fortnight the town of Victoria was growing. Twenty-four cottages, a hospital and officers' quarters were well under way....
>
> But too soon Bremer was withdrawn to fight the shameful Opium War.... A cyclone swept the settlement, dysentery, influenza, scurvy, malaria. Termites ate the fruit trees. Ants carried away vegetable seeds as soon as they were sown.[160]

Such a fate was far from restricted to the tropical north. However, the rout of the white colonists was complete up here. The abolishment of the idea of a transcontinental infrastructure, improved shipping links with Britain thus enabling the metropolis to assert its control over trade, and a general shift in attention from exploration of the inland to

159. It is interesting that in Australian literature it is possible to trace a strong and far more ambivalent narrative strand about the blessings of colonial and 'post-colonial' modernity. Margaret Simons's novel *The Ruthless Garden* is just one and a not particularly well-known example among many, but its narration of the chronology of progress-obsessed leaders of a godforsaken town in the Riverina, while salination is slowly killing the community, is a brilliant illustration of Australian modernity's dark shadows.

160. *Sojourners*, p. 256.

the goldfields in the southeast, were three important reasons why the embracing of Australia's location in the strategically important southeast corner of Asia was abandoned in favour of a view of Australia as a vulnerable British satellite in a volatile Asian backwater. The apprehension of the empty land worked primarily as a vehicle for fears of invasion by 'yellow hordes', through the almost literal image of people spilling down the map from an overpopulated north. Yet, the empty land was also regarded as a safety guard, a buffer zone between the majority of settlements which lay in the southern parts of the continent and the Asian countries, buttressed on the seas by the impregnable British navy.

Direct political involvement in Asian affairs was negligible until Australia's hand was forced by the events of the 1930s and 40s. Arguably, the imperial-colonial axis had prevented the colonies from executing any independent policy, since they were under the jurisdiction of the British Government. Besides a collective colonial Australian outlook was hindered by the intense rivalry, even animosity, between the colonies. After Australia's formal independence in 1901 its international relations continued to comply with the wishes of the British foreign office. However, the idea of Australia as an unfortunately isolated British-Irish derived enclave in the South Pacific came to an involuntary end with World War II. The single most important event was the fall of Singapore, which effectually punctured the myth of Britain as the guarantor of Australia's sovereignty. The Japanese capture of Singapore set in train a whole chain of events that redefined Australia's policies towards its Asian neighbours. Earlier signs of a break-up in the close affiliation between Australia and Britain can be located, for example in the Australian dissatisfaction with its treatment during World War I and in the sense of betrayal over the behaviour of the British during the Depression,[161] yet

161. John Rickard comments in his *Australia: A Cultural History* (Melbourne: Longman Cheshire, 1988) that a new orientation of Australia's regional role had taken place, and quotes Menzies's appointment speech as Prime Minister (p. 199). This new departure is, also according to Rickard, a reluctant one based on 'the realisation that British concern with European events might be at the expense of Australian — and imperial interests in the Pacific region' (pp. 199-200).

it is the collapse of Singapore that represents the point-of-no-return which forces a radically new departure. The focus shifted from the European to the Pacific theatre of war. Yet, as David Day points out in *Claiming a Continent* this did not lead to a reorientation in Australia's outlook at the end of the war:

> Although the Allies had successfully repelled Japan's wartime lunge towards Australia, the end of the war did not lay to rest Australia's fear of Asia. Only isolated voices argued for Australia to engage in meaningful dialogue with Asia and develop trade relations as the surest way of averting a future threat.[162]

Day's point shows that rather than the nation making the most of its newly won international independence, Australian intervention in Asia generally, and in Indonesia particularly came only when its hand was forced. Hence it was Australian troops which had recaptured the eastern part of the Indonesian archipelago at the end of World War II. The situation in Indonesia was extremely volatile and complex. The Japanese had encouraged the formation of an independent Indonesia towards the end of the war in the hope that it would stall the Allied advancement, but independent Indonesia was not recognised anywhere abroad, while Japanese troops were technically in charge until the arrival of Allied troops. In some parts the Japanese surrendered control to the Indonesians, in other parts to the Allied, who brought the Dutch colonists back. The 50,000 Australian soldiers in Indonesia were caught up in this situation too, and bound by their allied commitment they passed control back to the Dutch colonists. This obviously suggests an unproblematic alliance with the British and the Americans. However, in the subsequent negotiations for transfer of government from the Dutch to the Indonesians, Australia took a different attitude, when it expressed its sympathy for the Indonesians' demand for independence.

In his introduction to *Documents on Australian Foreign Policy 1937-49,* Philip Dorling opens with the following statement concerning Australia's role in the decolonisation of

162. Day, p. 347.

Indonesia after World War II: 'Indonesia's independence was an early and critical test of Australia's capacity to respond positively to change in Asia.'[163] Although a fear of Indonesian disintegration followed by waves of refugees may have had much to do with Australia's engagement, Australia, for whatever reason, came to play an active part in the Indonesian struggle to attain independence. Australia's involvement gave rise to considerable irritation in the British and American governments (which both supported the Dutch), even if the Australian support for Indonesian independence was far from unequivocal. Hence when a UN investigation into the Dutch-Indonesian conflict was proposed, Australia followed suit with its traditional allies and voted against.[164] Yet, if the policy was not consistently pro-Indonesian it was sufficiently so to provoke the Dutch to exclude Australia from the negotiations over Indonesia that were taking place. The obstinacy of the Dutch finally led to an outburst, albeit not a public one from the representatives abroad, to Canberra:

> The incomprehensible Dutch made formal protest yesterday at our offer to assist rehabilitation Indonesia. If they think now there is measure agreement with Indonesia...that they can reinstate pre-war exclusive trading policy they should know this will recreate trouble in Indonesia and also with rest of world. Indonesians urgently require economic assistance and advice and we propose trying to make it available.[165]

---

163. Introduction to *Documents on Australian Foreign Policy 1937-49, Vol. 11,* ed. by Philip Dorling (Canberra: Australian Government Publishing Service, 1975).

164. It is possible to argue that the wavering course reflected a basic shift from a belief in the possible resurrection of Dutch colonialism to a belief in independence as the only option. Furthermore, it has been a long established Australian foreign policy outlook that Indonesia must be kept together virtually at all costs, primarily one suspects because of Australian anxiety that a break-up would lead to masses of refugees descending on Australia. As such, the fear of the 'yellow hordes' continues to hold sway over Australian perceptions of Asia. In the same vein it rejected military intervention, much as the Howard government was to initially refuse committing Australian troops to East Timor at the end of the century.

165. *Documents...*, Document 115.

What lay behind Australia's final support for Indonesian independence was an overriding concern to preserve Indonesia as one nation, both in the early period when the Australian government supported the return of Dutch colonial power, and later when Australia shifted its allegiances to the Indonesian independence movement.[166] Australia's altered position was influenced by the realisation that the decolonisation of Indonesia was a foregone conclusion. Yet the change in policy was also due to the unsustainable attitude and actions of an oppressive Dutch colonial administration, and finally domestic pressure played an instrumental role. The Australian Labor government was placed in a delicate position, when the waterfront workers boycotted Dutch ships in Australian ports. Also in this case it would appear, as it is pointed out in *Documents,* that the Australian government was prevented from pursuing a policy of non-involvement in the conflict,[167] rather than seeking to play an active role on its own accord.

Australia's involvement during the Indonesian decolonisation phase is unique in so far as it brought Australia temporarily into an unlikely circle of Asian allies, while it alienated Australian relations with its traditional European and American allies. This happened to such an extent that Australia's actions were 'seen to be "in opposition throughout to Western interests."'[168] While this was not something to be morally concerned about, it obviously raised concerns about Australia's security, which was seen as inalienable from American and British foreign policy. The contradiction between the Australian realisation that it did not automatically share the same regional interests as Britain and the U.S., and the necessity of preserving in particular American goodwill has

166. See *Documents,* where the telegram sent back from the first Australian diplomat to visit Indonesia after World War II warned that 'Dutch Sovereignty is likely to be precarious, the ill-will between the Dutch and Indonesians so bitter and deep-rooted, that the NEI will be a focus of conflict between East and West. And from that focus the infection may spread with menacing speed to many other countries in South-East Asia' (p. x). This telegram reveals that the concern was less about who ruled Indonesia and more about ensuring Indonesia's integrity, as well as the usual fear of communism outside Australia's backdoor.

167. *Documents...*, p. x.

168. *Documents...*, vol. 2, p. xi.

continued to demarcate Australia's international outlook since, with a remarkable continuity. Australian right-wing governments have endlessly reiterated the double blessing of a nostalgic relationship with Britain and the 'naturalness' of having common interests with the United States. Australian Labor governments have in recent decades pursued a far more active policy, in particular in its relations with Indonesia, yet this is not necessarily evidence of a more progressive policy *per se.* Hence the policy with regards to the East Timor question has demonstrated a remarkable level of continuity in spite of changing governments. Both in terms of Whitlam's encouragement of the Indonesian take-over, in the subsequent refusal by Australian governments to condemn the Indonesian genocide of the East Timorese, and finally in the flexing of muscles as a regional power to secure the lion's share of the resources in the Timor Gap.

Yet there are also differences between Keating's and Howard's approach to the Indonesian relations, which are important in the context of this Chapter's concern with the forms Australian relations with Asia take. Hence the development of particularly the Keating Labor government's policy *vis-a-vis* Indonesia has been built around the idea of mutual respect and a personal relationship between particularly Suharto and Keating in the early 1990s. This has placed an Australian government, eager to present itself as progressive, in embarrassing situations in international forums, when it has had to defend its dealings with a dictatorship that has not only brutally oppressed opposition for most of its life as an independent nation, but which is also structured around an unmitigated presidential greediness which finally brought about his fall. On the other hand the Howard government's distancing of itself from Asian concerns, except when it comes to keeping refugees away from Australian shores and securing Australia's economic interests has on a number of occasions landed the Liberal government in equally embarrassing positions.

East Timor as a Case

The contradictions between continuity and change in Australia's political attitudes to Indonesia are no more apparent than in the thorny case of East Timor. I am not concerned here with examining the reasons for Indonesia's decision to invade East Timor, or the legitimacy of the East Timorese demand for independence, only in so far as they pertain to the arguments put forward in the Australian responses to the East Timor crisis. Instead I will focus on the three issues that have been the most important indicators of the kind of trouble faced by various Australian governments; the period leading up to the Indonesian invasion; the Timor Gap Treaty; and the crisis in East Timor in connection with the vote for self-determination in 1999.

The assessment may appear to invite a chronological survey of Australian responses to East Timor, but in interesting ways they have actually been circular, and it is my contention that their circularity is evidence of inadequately developed responses that continue to come back and haunt Australian policy makers.[169]

My attention was brought to the importance of the East Timor question to Australian international politics, when I read a vicious outburst from former Prime Minister Gough Whitlam in a letter to the editors published in *The Age* (October 31, 1998). In this letter Whitlam angrily rejects that he as Prime Minister had any direct or indirect responsibility for the Indonesian invasion on December 7, 1975, or for the killing of five journalists (among whom two were Australians) at Balibo in East Timor on October 16, 1975. The angry response of the former Prime Minister is a clear indication of the volatile status not only of Australia's relations with Indonesia, but also of the emotional investment in Australia's involvement with Indonesia. One of the more recent emotional eruptions in connection with the same crisis followed in the wake of the Sherman report into the killing of the 5 Western journalists at Balibo in East Timor. The Indonesians claimed that the five journalists were killed in crossfire between FRETILIN and Indonesian backed Timorese militias in October 1975. A

169. I am aware that the self-interest of the Australian governments, for instance in relation to securing Australia's maximum share of the rich oil resources in the Timor Gap have led to reassessments and turnabouts in Australian policy, but the point here is to inquire into Australian governments' revelation of their attitudes to Australia's geopolitical position.

whole range of books and articles have told a different story: That in fact Indonesia was in the full process of invading East Timor already in October 1975, two months before the official invasion date; that the journalists were recording this on film, and to prevent media exposure of their illicit invasion the Indonesians killed them.[170] The Australian government did not pursue the matter with the Indonesians, but officially accepted the story about accidental killings. Hence it took twenty years before a detailed inquiry was carried out.[171]

Whitlam in his defence of his actions as Prime Minister made use of the Sherman report to deny that he owed any apology 'to the people of East Timor since I "passively accepted the Indonesian invasion" in 1975' and stated categorically that 'There is nothing in [the report] for which I, or any Australian now or formerly in official positions, should say sorry'.[172] Whitlam then comes, at least in that context, with a curious comment, namely that 'the Menzies Government found that East Timor was economically unviable. All subsequent Australian governments have agreed.'[173] The comment is curious

170. No one seriously contests the evidence that the Indonesian military executed these five journalists, although several Western governments have done their utmost to cover up what they have known all along.

171. An inquiry which when it was finally established had to work under its own restrictions as Maureen Tolfree argues:

> From 1995 on, the cover-up began to unravel. At Lord Avebury's request, James Dunn produced a report — published simultaneously in Australia and Britain on the 20th anniversary of the killings — entitled *Timor: the Balibo Incident in Perspective....* It then became possible for East Timorese participants in the covert Indonesian invasion force to speak publicly about some of what they knew. At that point, Australia's Labour government quickly set up what they saw as a 'damage-limitation' exercise: Tom Sherman's preliminary evaluation of evidence about the deaths of the five newsmen at Balibo... (Maureen Tolfree, 'Balibo: The Cover-up that Led to Genocide', in *The East Timor Question: The Struggle for Independence from Indonesia,* ed. by Paul Hainsworth and Stephen McCloskey (London: I.B. Tauris & Co. Ltd., 2000), p. 48.

172. *The Age,* October 31, 1998.

173. Whitlam's statement is almost identical to the Portuguese fascist leader Salazar who comments in a letter to Menzies in 1963: 'Given the fact that Timor cannot be an independent State, the territory either continues to be a part of Portugal as an autonomous province that it is or is

because it argues that the Indonesian invasion was in East Timor's own interests. Yet had this been the case, the Indonesians could have been invited as friends instead of invaders, unless Whitlam really thinks that the Indonesians were concerned about the East Timorese. How that is supposed to be connected to what amounts to a genocide[174] after the invasion is beyond rational thinking. Furthermore, Whitlam had not needed to draw attention to the subsequent endorsement of the Indonesian invasion by Australian governments, he could simply have drawn attention to his own statement as Prime Minister in 1974, where he acknowledged to the Indonesians 'that the best option for Portuguese Timor was connection with Indonesia.'[175] In this instance also there seemed to be little need to concern oneself with what the East Timorese themselves might think. Finally, Whitlam lays the full blame at the door of 'the pusillanimous and perfidious Portuguese' who did not protest to the Security Council after October 16, and who fled from Timor 'after culpably neglecting the people for four centuries'. This statement leads Whitlam to the curious position of accusing a

---

annexed to the Republic of Indonesia' [*Australia and the Indonesian Incorporation of Portuguese Timor 1974-1976* ed. by Wendy Way (Melbourne: Melbourne University Press, 2000, p. 29)]. Hence the excuse of a fascist defending his right to empire, is identical to that of a democratically elected leader refusing to acknowledge the inalienable right to self-determination.

174. The proportion of the East Timorese population killed outnumbers the figures for both Rwanda and Cambodia.

175. See Henry S. Albinski, *Australian External Policy under Labor: Content, Process and The National Debate* (Vancouver: University of British Columbia Press, 1977), p. 107. An even more damaging record of Whitlam's East Timor intervention emerges from one of the secret reports released in *Australia and the Indonesian Incorporation of Portuguese Timor 1974-1976* from Woolcott:

> Particularly important to the Indonesians was the Prime Minister's view [during Whitlam's meeting with Soeharto in Townsville, April 1975] expressed in the Record as follows: 'He wished to reaffirm, however, that we strongly desired closer and more cordial relations with Indonesia and would ensure that our actions in regard to Portuguese Timor would always be guided by the principle that good relations with Indonesia were of paramount importance to Australia'. (p. 469)

fascist European empire of inadequate colonisation. Whitlam furthermore omits to mention that during the decolonisation era after World War II, Portugal had been led by a fascist regime, whose fall in 1974 eventually brought in a Marxist-led government, which began a decolonisation process that had already gained momentum elsewhere in the Portuguese Empire, through the African colonial wars and had already influenced the East Timorese nationalist movement, at the time when Whitlam is unconcerned with their response.

However, Whitlam's errand here has less to do with any interest in East Timor, for his conflation of events and periods serves a different and very particular purpose here: To deflect attention from his own foreign policy in the period leading up to the Indonesian invasion. To consider the context in which Whitlam's actions have to be placed, we turn to a paper, 'Indonesia and Australia: Political Aspects', which he delivered at a conference in 1990. In this paper Whitlam offers his views on what happened in the period before and after the Indonesian invasion, and his points may in chronological order be outlined as follows:

(a) Whitlam begins by asserting his determination, when he was elected, to 'restore the trusting relations with Indonesia which Australia had established in the late 1940s'. Whitlam holds the view that the arguments of the opposition in the 1940s were racist in nature, and implicitly he argues that relations between Australia and Indonesia waned in the interim period between Chifley's and his own government,

(b) he emphasises Suharto's reluctance in invading East Timor.

Furthermore he argues

(c) that the Timorese 'leaders were mostly *mesticos* who had spent some time in seminaries and the army and who often seemed to be desperate to succeed the Portuguese as rulers over the rest of the population',

(d) that 'President Suharto and I agreed that Portugal should be encouraged to maintain her authority in Timor for some time longer, probably five years, in order to give the population some experience in managing its affairs',

(e) that 'we were to be frustrated in this by the irresponsibility of the Portuguese and the intransigence of the parties',

(f) that 'on 28 November Fretilin proclaimed the Democratic Republic of East Timor; the nomenclature had overtones of East Germany, North Korea and North Vietnam',

(g) then Whitlam goes on to implicitly blame Fretilin for civilian deaths by citing without comment or documentary evidence an opposition spokesperson's accusation. The Indonesians features nowhere in this picture of violence,

(h) finally, 'the Portuguese had been the first imperialists from Europe to reach the East Indies and the last to leave. Their departure was not only more ignominious and pusillanimous but more swift and bloody than that of the Dutch or British'.[176]

Whitlam seeks to argue through a chronological presentation of events that the Portuguese and the communists (whom he equates squarely with the FRETILIN movement) share the blame for the Indonesian invasion. Behind Whitlam's stance lurks the unstated argument that East Timor is unsustainable as a nation, unstated because it runs counter to the UN position, but also one suspects because it becomes increasingly clear to Whitlam that East Timor will become a nation. Yet there are other strategic interests behind the East Timor question, which necessarily compromise the Australian international stance: the stability of Indonesia, the fear of a left-wing led independent East Timor and access to the seabed resources in the strait between Australia and Indonesia/East Timor (what subsequently becomes known as the Timor Gap). Before turning to consider these wider issues I wish to briefly counter a few of Whitlam's statements, in the interest of setting the record straight.

---

176. *Australia and the Indonesian Incorporation of Portuguese Timor 1974-1976*, ed. by Wendy Way (Melbourne: Melbourne U.P., 2000), pp. 755-57.

First of all, it would appear that he has read none of the numerous books on East Timor which have emerged since 1980. In these books he would find a vastly more detailed, and very different version of events from the one he presents. If we begin with his reading of Indonesia's role and intention it is clear (as it should be to Whitlam through the intelligence sources quoted, which would presumably be available to an Australian Prime Minister) that Indonesia did in actuality invade parts of East Timor months prior to the official invasion on December 7.

Secondly, although Suharto may have been reluctant to authorise the invasion, the army was extremely eager to press forward, but one of the important obstacles was the American opposition to the use of their weaponry during the invasion. If Suharto was against how could the *de facto* invasion go on for months without his intervention? Even if we look at the official invasion in isolation, the Whitlam record also runs into problems. Although as Whitlam points out, the invasion took place when he had been replaced by Fraser, Whitlam had had a meeting with Suharto in September 1974, which John Taylor in *Indonesia's Forgotten War* recounts as follows:

> During their discussions in Wonosobo, Suharto tentatively raised the subject of East Timor and was staggered by Whitlam's resolute answer. The Australian prime minister was fully briefed, personally involved and disarmingly forthright: 'An independent East Timor would be an unviable state, and a potential threat to the area', he said.[177]

These are the exact words Whitlam used in his letter to the editor that I quoted earlier, but in the latter case Whitlam was unable to make the link to the Indonesian invasion. Or to be more precise he would have found it difficult to express that an Australian Labor government could condone the invasion of a small nation on the grounds that it might otherwise have

177. John G. Taylor, *Indonesia's Forgotten War; The Hidden History of East Timor* (London: Zed Books, 1991), p. 32. The quotation from Whitlam is from *The Sydney Morning Herald*, November 19th, 1974.

established a radical left-wing state.[178] There is, however, little doubt that this consideration weighed heavily on the minds of all active and passive participants in the destruction of East Timor's independence.

The other point to consider in Whitlam's presentation of events is his representation of the East Timorese themselves, for it is in fact remarkably consistent with that of all subsequent Australian governments. Speaking of the handle with kid gloves approach of Australian governments to Indonesia over East Timor, *The Age's* foreign editor, Tom Hyland, wryly observes that 'Australia's coyness towards Jakarta contrasts sharply with the tone of official remarks towards the East Timorese, who are portrayed as faction-ridden and troublesome'.[179] Hyland quotes Alexander Downer who 'lamented that the East Timorese aren't "more saintly", as if their torment was of their own making'.[180] Hyland's observation on the continuity in Australia's response to the East Timor question is borne out by the former foreign minister, Gareth Evans, who in an interview on Radio National, March 3, 1999, said that 'Downer's been reasonably well advised, professionally...and I've got no particular quarrel with the way the issue is being handled right now'.[181] How could he since the Liberal government pursued the same policy as the Labor government on East

178. It is worth remembering that a radical left-wing government was the norm among nationalist movements in the former Lusophone colonies, and that leading figures in the pan-Lusophone nationalist movement such as Amilcar Cabral had in mind precisely the kind of self-determination which was envisaged by the independence movement in East Timor. Furthermore to label activities by the leaders of the independence movement as suspicious because they were 'mesticos' is an extremely derogatory remark bordering on racism. Unless of course one is to see this as a kind of cultural limitation these leaders suffered due to their education in thoughts pertaining to a European universe. However, by the same token one could argue that most Australian politicians could be labelled in much the same way.

179. Tom Hyland, 'Our Whispering Leaders', article in *The Age*, April 20, 1999.

180. *The Age*, April 20, 1999.

181. It is important to note that Evans spoke in the context of internal criticism in the Labor Party over the way the East Timor case had been handled, during Labor's years in power.

Timor, and precisely for the same reasons. Downer's remarks about the pro-independence movement in East Timor are no less critical than Whitlam's attempt to portray the independence movement as unrepresentative and illegitimate, through the reference to the movement's mixed background [*mesticos* (b)], dictatorial inclinations [(c, e, g) with no evidence given to back him up), and that the loss of life is somehow due to the East Timorese themselves (ignoring in that comment the abundance of evidence which proves the Indonesian genocide (g)]. The official rhetoric of Whitlam, Evans and Downer suggests there is little leeway for humanitarian concerns with regards to the East Timorese, when it collides with the overriding desire of securing Indonesia's integrity[182] (but also with Australia's economic interest in the seabed). This approach is governed by a view that may be summed up as did the parliamentary committee on Australia's relations with Indonesia, which concluded 'it is still true that Indonesia matters more to Australia than the reverse'.[183] The lack of self-confidence betrayed by such an attitude shows a sense of continual existence on the margins, as if Australia's 'Asian

---

182. In fact such a reading is supported by the findings of the Joint Standing Committee on Foreign Affairs (published in 1993). The committee pointed out that:

> it could be argued that there were few options open to various Australian governments since 1975. It could also be argued that the granting by Australia of *de facto* recognition of the incorporation of East Timor on 21 January 1978 and *de jure* recognition on 22 December 1978 were so hasty as to imply condonation of Indonesia's action or, in many eyes, should never have been given. [The Parliament of the Commonwealth of Australia; Joint Standing Committee on Foreign Affairs, Defence and Trade, *Australia's Relations with Indonesia* (Canberra: Australian Government Publishing Service, November 1993, p. 105)].

If this part of the committee's conclusions reflected the duality inherent in Australia's policy on East Timor, the criticism of the human rights record was more equivocal:

> while this country has a laudable history of promoting human rights and condemning human rights abuses in distant parts of the world, by softening the EC's strongly worded resolution on the killings in Dili, Australia lessened its credibility on the issue of human rights in Indonesia. (p. 106)

183. Joint Standing Committee on Foreign Affairs, p. 106.

turn' merely represents a transformation from a European to an Asian satellite. Yet, if Australian politics in cultural terms are weak, it is a very different degree of self-confidence that marks Australia's far more embracing outlook on Indonesia and East Timor in economic terms. A fact that is expressed through the Timor Gap Treaty which merits a few observations.

To begin with the Parliamentary committee, it found that 'The Treaty is an unusual and constructive resolution of a boundary issue and is seen as a milestone in improving the bilateral relationship'.[184] If this suggests an unproblematic negotiation over a delicate issue, the committee does include statements by people who were critical of the treaty, because it was negotiated without the acceptance of the East Timorese, despite the fact that it lay within their territorial boundaries, since only Australia officially recognised Indonesia's incorporation of East Timor. This criticism may be summed up by Shirley Shackleton statement that:

> the Treaty [is] 'illegal'...it has made Australia a party to the expropriation of ocean resources critically important to the East Timor economy. She had reason to believe the Treaty had given rise to a perception among Australians of deep shame and loss of self-respect, preventing the establishment of sound relations with Indonesia at the most fundamental level.... That Portugal has taken Australia to the International Court of Justice over this issue is a continuing humiliation.[185]

The committee's resolution on humanitarian issues is considerably weakened when it comes to the Treaty, and it concludes rather lamely that 'while there has been concerns raised about the signing of the Timor Gap Treaty, it represents a cooperative solution to part of the boundary and resource problems between Australia and Indonesia.'[186] The conclusion is particularly weak because the Treaty's legitimacy rests on the assumption of the Indonesian government's right to negotiate on behalf of the East Timorese, and that together

184. Joint Standing Committee on Foreign Affairs, p. 185.

185. Joint Standing Committee on Foreign Affairs, p. 187.

186. Joint Standing Committee on Foreign Affairs, p. 190.

with Australia Indonesia will reap the economic benefits expected from the resources in the Gap. And the conclusion is further undermined when held against the fact that Australia has so far refused to honour the UN Convention on the Law of the Sea (from December 1982, ratified by the necessary 60 member states to become effective in 1994), which would lead to a far better deal for East Timor as far as economic benefits from the oil and gas reserves are concerned.[187] Another scandal has brewed over the Howard government's handling of the independence vote crisis, with accusations that the intervention when it came served mainly to secure Australia's economic interests, and after the departure of the Indonesians, whereas in effect the government had been warned months before that a carnage would follow in the wake of the referendum.[188] It is difficult to escape the conclusion that even if the Indonesian withdrawal from East Timor has let Australia off an embarrassing hook, Australia continues to be unable to articulate a more self-confident approach to understanding its own position in the geopolitical environment of Southeast Asia. If the specific contextualisation of Australia in cultural-political terms here leads to a disappointing conclusion concerning the ability to actually articulate a more culturally embedded (and indeed informed) response to local crises, this needs also to be seen in the light of the Australian context as a self-defined transplanted Western culture.

The Broader Picture

The joint parliamentary committee's views quoted earlier may be seen as a broader reflection on trends in Western democracies to emphasise humanitarian issues, when they are relatively free of charge, while economic considerations are encouraged with little hesitation. This separation between human rights and economic interests are thus not unique to

187. See Joseph Nevins, 'A Dangerous Oil Slick: Australia Tries to Hijack East Timor's Future' (Vol. 8, no. 1, Spring 2002), www.etan.org/estafeta/02/spring02/4gap.html.

188. For focus on the timing of Australia's intervention into East Timor, see Mike Head, 'East Timor and Australia's Oily Politics' (*World Socialist Web Site,* March 8, 2000), www.wsws.org.articles/2000/mar2000/timo-m08/shtml.

Australia, but because of Australia's proximity to Southeast Asian countries with limited respects for their citizens' rights, the Australian predicament is often more directly exposed. While that can be used as an argument for delimitating what Australia can afford to do in its dealings with its Southeast Asian neighbours as has often been the case, the question is also where such an approach will lead Australia. Hence as it is pointed in the Introduction to *Pathways to Asia*:

> Conservative Asian leaders (Lee Kwan Yew, Mahathir and Soeharto) have argued that 'Asian' models of political and social organisation embody the principles of harmony, hierarchy and consensus. This they contrast to the confrontation, individualism and decay that characterises Western liberalism.... By claiming an immutable and discrete Asian set of values, conservative leaders are able to deny legitimacy to domestic opponents, who can be dismissed as opposing the national interest or simply being un-Asian. The cultural relativism implicit in their claims can be used to deny the validity of any non-Asian (or even non-national) judgements upon such issues as human rights.[189]

The implicit danger in taking such a position is clear, the question is to what extent that has not already been the one held throughout the East Timor debacle. Furthermore, before East Timor it would appear that the same attitude governed Australia's engagement in the Vietnam War, although here the public opposition was far more pervasive and radically expressed.

On the Asian side of the equation the argument for essential Asian values are used to legitimise a high degree of interaction between government and industry, corporate government if you like. Any internal opposition to such a value system becomes both anti-Asian value, anti-democratic, and a threat against national economic interests. This creates two related problems. The first pertains to essentialising a particular set of values as 'Asian', which runs against the idea of a pluralist democracy and certainly rejects alternative versions of 'Asian

189. *Pathways to Asia: The Politics of Engagement*, ed. by Richard Robison (Sydney: Allen & Unwin, 1996), p. 4.

values', if indeed it makes any sense to speak of these, other than as a counterweight to Western influence. The second point, I wish to make, is related to this, for it is an open question, whether the values celebrated by the conservative Asian leaders, are particularly Asian:

> Liberalism, communism and social democracy have all played important roles in modern Asian history along with the sort of Hegelian authoritarianism claimed by Asian conservatives to embody the essence of Asia.... Such movement and diversity within Asia undermines the claims of Lee, Soeharto and others about Asian values. Their caricature of an 'Asian' press is a case in point. Rigorous control of information and media is not a general Asian phenomenon.[190]

With this questioning of the 'Asian reality' supposedly represented by these conservative Asian value systems, I will consider the implications of such a questioning in an Australian context.

The conservative Asian leaders have participated in the Australian debate to an extent that would hardly have been appreciated had the situation been the reverse, which speaks volumes not about Asian values, but about the authoritarian base of most governments in South East Asia. Hence the Malaysian Prime Minister, Mahathir, has argued 'that Australia must become more like "Asia" if it is to successfully engage.'[191] Whatever Mahathir may be thinking of specifically, the reality is that Australia is located geographically in a region, where labour conditions are vastly different from the Australian ones. The reality is also, however, that there is extensive cooperation between governments and business in the region, so the response to the Asian challenge is not necessarily only gaucho economics (or rampant capitalism), and unmitigated deregulation of protective Labor market conditions. Yet, this is precisely what the Australian governments have seized upon:

> Since the industry plans of the 1980s Australian policymakers have studiously avoided and even denied

190. *Pathways to Asia*, pp. 16-17.

191. *Pathways to Asia*, p. 5.

> those dimensions of Asian economic development involving planning in industry and trade and institutional cooperation between government and business. Upon this conclusion they confirm that the appropriate policy for engagement with the new global economy and with Asia is one of deregulation of the Australian economy. In other words, their interest in the Asian experience is primarily aimed at substantiating an existing agenda.[192]

The way of responding to the Asian challenge is not unique to Australia, but has developed in remarkably similar fashion in Europe, where corporate management is gradually replacing/ eroding political leadership in euphemistically disguised terminology as The Third Way. The main difference is the extensive cooperation between European nations in the EU, which as a block is able to introduce protective measures, interestingly enough while the national governments are removing them. Australia is obviously in a more exposed position, but the point I am making here, is that governments do have choices, that is why they were elected, and the choices they make, reflect a set of political values that are not simply forced upon them by external forces, although such forces exert pressures:

> The neo-liberal pathway offers solutions to governments increasingly unable to fund traditional social democratic budgets or to insulate economies from international pressures, particularly on the price of labor.... What is perhaps unique about the shift to neo-liberalism in Australia is that it has been done in the name of preserving social democracy.[193]

As I have indicated this is not unique to Australia, as the vast majority of social democratic governments pursuing the same policies in the EU testifies, but it did happen in Australia before it happened in Europe. The necessity of such policies can then be seen in the light of the Australian experience, and it is difficult to escape the conclusion, that there are more options than those used by the Australian governments

---

192. *Pathways to Asia*, p. 13.

193. *Pathways to Asia*, pp. 21-22.

to counter neo-liberalism. Hence the Hawke/Keating Labor axis has created more millionaires than any Liberal government.[194] Of course, this does not mean that Howard has not done his best to emulate the achievement of the previous Labor governments, but it does invite the question where anti-neo-liberal forces can expect their views to be represented, as the differences between Liberal and Labor governments become increasingly negligible. This is an important question if the idea of democracy 'is principally about the legitimacy of the power of ordinary people to exercise some kind of control over political elites and to judge the appropriateness of policy decisions made on their behalf that can vitally effect their lives'.[195]

If Australia is to gain credibility as a partner for the South East Asian countries, what is the right approach? The record in the postwar period has hardly been impressive. While its participation in the Vietnam War, its obliging silence on the East Timor question,[196] may be seen as constructive by its

194. For a lengthy study of the effects of neo-liberalism on Australia see John Wiseman, *Global Nation? Australia and the Politics of Globalisation* (Cambridge: Cambridge U.P., 1998), and for an assessment in particular on Labor deregulation see pp. 42-48.

195. *Pathways to Asia*, p. 124.

196. Gareth Evans has defended his record as Foreign Minister by dismissing accusations that:

> Australia's performance on human rights during my term of office as Foreign Minister, in East Timor or anywhere else, 'fell short of the high ideals and standards we profess to hold dear'. I did often make the judgement that it was more productive to work behind the scenes rather than with grandstanding rhetoric (Press release, February 4, 1999).

Yet Evans's distinction is hardly borne out by his policy record on East Timor as outlined by Tom Hyland:

> We are virtually alone in formally recognising Indonesia's sovereignty over East Timor, despite the Timorese people's enduring resistance to Jakarta's rule. We have defended Jakarta in the UN. We have often sought to soften international criticism of its human rights record in such international forums as the UN Human Rights Commission. When the United States downgraded its defence cooperation with Indonesia after the 1991 Dili massacre, the Australian military quickly filled the gap. (Tom Hyland, *The Age*, April 20, 1999)

conservatively led trading partners (in so far as they can readily identify with such politics), this has serious consequences for its internal credibility as well as for its international standing. Already under siege for its handling of the Aboriginal land rights issue, its speedy recognition of the Indonesian colonisation of East Timor, and its inability to criticise Indonesian abuses of human rights, the polarisation between its international humanitarian record and its status as a democratic government, may lead to a threat to democracy. Eruptions such as Pauline Hanson and her One Nation is an illustrative case, anti-Asian, anti-Aboriginal, and anti-rampant Capitalism (particularly its consequences for the rural poor), with a fuzzy tissue of unconnected ideas, this party trades in identifying the issues that are driven like wedges into the Australian society, and which threaten to undermine its social cohesiveness, even as it identifies these threats as cultural rather than economic. A better response is needed than to characterise such movements as those of the loony few, and the continuation of the practice of paying lipservice to what has so grossly inaccurately been labelled the international community.

REFERENCES

Internet sources: htto://www.garethevans.dynamite.com.au

Albinski, Henry S., *Australian External Policy under Labor: Content, Process and The National Debate* (Vancouver: University of British Columbia Press, 1977).

Alter/Asians: Asian-Australian Identities in Art, Media and Popular Culture, ed. by Ien Ang, Sharon Chalmers, Lisa Law and Mandy Thomas (Sydney: Pluto Press, 2000).

Akashi, Yoji, *The East Timor Question in Australian-Indonesian Relations: An Australian Perception* (Nagoya, Japan: Narzan University, 1995).

Anderson, Benedict R. O'G., *Language and Power: Exploring Political Cultures in Indonesia* (New York: Cornell U.P., 1990).

Australia and the Indonesian Incorporation of Portuguese Timor 1974-1976 ed. by Wendy Way (Melbourne: Melbourne University Press, 2000).

Australia in World Affairs 1961-1965, ed. by Gordon Greenwood and Norman Harper (London: Angus and Robertson, 1968).

Broinowsky, Alison, *The Yellow Lady: Australian Impressions of Asia* (Melbourne: Oxford U.P., 1992).

Brown, Nicholas, 'Australian Intellectuals and the Image of Asia: 1920-1960', in *Australian Perceptions of Asia. Special Issue of Australian Cultural*

History, no. 9, 1990 ed. by David Walker, Julian Horne and Adrian Vickers, pp. 80-92.

Carey, Peter and G. Carter Bentley (eds.), *East Timor at the Crossroads: The Forging of a Nation* (London: Cassell, 1995).

Catley, Robert, *Australian Indonesian Relations Since 1945: The Garuda and the Kangaroo* (Brookfield, Vic: Ashgate, 1998).

Comparing Cultures, ed. by Anthony Milner and Mary Quilty (Melbourne: Oxford U.P., 1996).

Cribb, Robert and Colin Brown, *Modern Indonesia: A History Since 1945* (London: Longman, 1995).

Dever, Maryanne (ed.), *Australia and Asia: Cultural Transactions* (Honolulu: University of Hawai'i Press, 1997).

Diaspora: Negotiating Asian-Australia ed. by Helen Gilbert, Tseen Khoo and Jacqueline Lo (St. Lucia: UQP, 2000).

Documents on Australian Foreign Policy 1937-49, (Canberra: Australian Government Publishing Service, 1975), Vol. XI, Indonesia 1947 ed. by Philip Dorling.

Edwards, P.G., *Prime Ministers and Diplomats: The Making of Australian Foreign Policy, 1901-1949* (Melbourne: Oxford U.P., 1983).

Evans, Gareth and Bruce Grant, *Australia's Foreign Relations in the World of the 1990s* (Melbourne: Melbourne University Press, 1992).

George, M., *Australia and the Indonesian Revolution* (Melbourne: Melbourne U.P., 1980).

Gerster, Robin (ed.), *Hotel Asia: An Anthology of Australian Literary Travelling to the 'East'* (Melbourne: Penguin, 1995).

Head, Mike, 'East Timor and Australia's Oily Politics, (*World Socialist Web Site,* March 8, 2000), www.wsws.org.articles/2000/mar2000/timo-m08/shtml.

Hyland, Tom, 'Our Whispering Leaders', *The Age,* April 20, 1999.

Indonesia: Australian Perspectives, vol. III: Indonesia: The Making of a Nation, ed. by JAC Mackie (Canberra: ANU, 1980).

Islam in an Era of Nation-States: Politics and Religious Renewal in Muslim Southeast Asia ed. by Robert W. Hefner and Patricia Horvatich (Honolulu: University of Hawai'i Press, 1997.

Jannisa, Gudmund, *The Crocodile's Tears; East Timor in the Making* (Lund: Lund U.P., 1997).

Kahin, George McTurnan, *Nationalism and Revolution in Indonesia* (Ithaca: Cornell U.P., 1952).

Legge, John (ed.), *New Directions in Australian Foreign Policy: Australia and Indonesia 1945-50* (Clayton: Monash U.P., 1997).

Lockwood, Rupert, *Black Armada: Australia and the Struggle for Indonesian Independence 1942-49* (Sydney: Hale and Iremonger, 1982).

Millar, T.B., *Australia in Peace and War* (Canberra: ANU Press, 1978).

Nevins, Joseph, 'A Dangerous Oil Slick: Australia Tries to Hijack East Timor's Future' (Vol. 8, no. 1, Spring 2002), www.etan.org/estafeta/02/spring02/4gap.html.

Pathways to Asia: The Politics of Engagement, ed. by Richard Robison (Sydney: Allen & Unwin, 1996).

Reid, A.J.S., *The Indonesian National Revolution* (Hawthorn: Longman, 1974).

Ramos-Horta, Jose, *Funu: The Unfinished Saga of East Timor* (New Jersey: The Red Sea Press, 1987).

Ricklefs, M.C., *A History of Modern Indonesia Since c. 1300* (London: Macmillan, 1993).

Rabbitt Roff, Sue, *Timor's Anschluss: Indonesia and Australian Policy in East Timor, 1974-76* (Lewiston: E. Mellen Press, 1992).

Report on the Deaths of Australian-based Journalists in East Timor in 1975 (The Sherman Report) Canberra: Australian Government Publications, June 1996).

Taylor, A.M., *Indonesian Independence and the United Nations* (Ithaca: Cornell U.P., 1960).

Taylor, John G., *Indonesia's Forgotten War: The Hidden History of East Timor* (London: Zed Books, 1991).

The East Timor Question: The Struggle for Independence from Indonesia, ed. by Paul Hainsworth and Stephen McCloskey (London: I.B. Tauris & Co Ltd., 2000).

The Parliament of the Commonwealth of Australia; Joint Standing Committee on Foreign Affairs, Defence and Trade, *Australia's Relations with Indonesia* (Canberra: Australian Government Publishing Service, November 1993).

Vandenbosch, MaryBelle and Amry, *Australia Faces Southeast Asia: The Emergence of a Foreign Policy* (Lexington: University of Kentucky Press, 1967).

Watt, Alan, *The Evolution of Australian Foreign Policy 1938-1965* (Cambridge: Cambridge U.P., 1967).

Yu, Ouyang, *Moon over Melbourne* (Melbourne: Papyrus Publishing, 1995).

4

Multiculturalism and the Chinese-Australians

> For certain people exile is the only tolerable condition.
> For those people to be in exile is to be home.
>
> (August Spiess in Alex Miller, *The Ancestor Game*)

The opening quotation addresses one of the central preoccupations in Australian literature; questions of belonging/ unbelonging and settlement vs. migration. Whereas European immigration into Australia in the nineteenth century is represented as settlement, whether they stayed or left (as many golddiggers did for example), the post-war influx of migrants from continental Europe, and later from the Middle East and Asia is generally discussed in relation to the concept of migrancy. This discrepancy between the preferred choice of words invites a closer investigation of the difference in meaning between the two terms. The term 'settlement' can imply a flux both in the settler, that is in his/her desires, anticipations and anxieties to reach a destiny, as well as an indeterminacy about the land whose meaning is still to be settled. Hence settlement can productively be understood as a process of negotiation between settler and place. The term 'migrant' signals a transition that takes place only in the migrant. S/he is seen to arrive in a place whose meaning is always already given.

Perhaps it is tempting to dismiss the differences between the terms as symbolic of the differences between nineteenth- and twentieth-century perceptions of migration. Or to point out the relatively recent arrival of non-British migrants, particularly Asian migrants who have arrived after the abolishment of the white Australia policy in the early 1970s. This is, however, to miss two important points. The first is that migrants did arrive from other places than the British Isles throughout the nineteenth century, when Australia according to conventional nationalist rhetoric was still 'being formed'. Significantly, it is the same nationalistic constructions that have written these non-British Isles migrants out of the national story, either by completely ignoring them or by strategically incorporating them into the monocultural bush ethos. The second point is related to the first, for behind the nationalistic constructions of Australian space operates an ideological perception that is both monocultural and exclusivist. According to this outlook Australia's identity was formed and indeed settled as simultaneously British derived and yet uniquely Australian by the end of the nineteenth century, and the devotion to Empire and confirmation of national identity sealed through the sacrifice of soldiers in the First World War.

Hence, when large-scale immigration began in earnest through the adoption of the post-war 'populate or perish', the field inside which Australian identity could be argued over had long since been 'settled'. Newcomers from other regions than the British Isles, the traditional suppliers of future Australians, were welcome to contribute to but could not be acknowledged as influencing or changing the Australian identity. Australia was seen as already formed with its own complete national mythology, represented for example in Russell Ward's detailed description of the typical (white) Australian (male), and in the general Australian pantheon of failed heroes from the convicts, to the golddiggers, explorers, the drovers and the shearers, reaching its fully fledged maturity in the First World War with the Anzacs. It is easy to see that such a nationalistic representation is far from representative. First of all it excludes women and Aborigines both from being representative and from exerting any influence on the form given to 'Australian identity'. Secondly, such a cast of national heroes disregards the fact that most people, also in Australian colonial times, were actually urbanised, and thirdly, it leaves out the fact that if one were to accept these hero-types they did include both Aboriginal war heroes,[197] Chinese bushrangers, and golddiggers from all over the world. Yet by 1938 a survey showed that Australians were 98 per cent British, and Prime Minister Lyons proudly proclaimed that Australia was more British than Britain. So, absurdly if migrants of a non-British background stayed long enough to be accepted as settlers they came to be counted not only as Australians, but also to be considered as of British stock.[198]

Today, to consider a British dimension in Australian identity would be a redundant exercise, yet what is worth considering is the question whether what it means to become an Australian in today's multicultural Australia, is still defined in deference to a nationalistic agenda? What does emerge as an immediate paradox is the fact that the transition from monocultural to multicultural Australia has been so relatively smooth. This is paradoxical because multiculturalism supposedly emphasises the multiple identity as a central ingredient in the make-up of an Australian identity, which (ought to) run counter to nationalistic constructions of Australian identity still trapped

197. Even if Aboriginal war heroes were to be included the irony does not stop here, as becomes clear if we mention Aborigines fighting in World War I and guerilla leaders from Pemulwuy in early colonial Sydney to the 1930s in Australia's north-west. It is to the credit of black Australian writers that these figures have been resurrected to once again challenge contemporary nationalistic constructions of Australia's colonial history.

198. In an otherwise disappointingly politically naïve reading of the evolution of multiculturalism in Australia, Mark Lopez does at least in this instance rise to the occasion: 'Claims about Australia being '98 per cent British' before World War II were exaggerations fabricated by counting as British, children born in Australia of non-British parents and persons from Empire territories like Hong Kong and Cyprus. Price argued in 1956 that, when the anomalies are corrected, as long back as 1900 the non-British element in Australia was as high as 9 per cent. In 1947, at the time the first displaced persons arrived, the level of ethnic diversity was as high as 11 per cent.' Mark Lopez, *The Origins of Multiculturalism in Australian Politics 1945-1975* (Melbourne: Melbourne University Press, 2000), p. 85. Lopez's account seeks to tread a fine balance between the pro-multiculturalist forces and the anti-multiculturalists, but unfortunately decides that the way to avoid the pitfalls of either 'camp' is to strive towards some mysterious idea of an apolitical approach. However, the book does represent the first thorough account of the process itself.

in the increasingly redundant images shaped by the legends of the bush, and the bloody sacrifice of two World Wars. Yet if this gap is widening, there is a constant supply of populists exploiting this gap to fill in their own antiquated and contradictory images of an Australian settlement to safeguard against two narrative strands in Australian history which they see as challenging to the national ethos: the multicultural make-up of Australia also in colonial times, and the displacement of the Aborigines' importance to successful farming, particularly in remote areas.

To go behind the artificial distinction between settlement and migrancy, it is necessary first to problematise the reification of a particular model of national identity, and secondly to investigate the nature of Australian multiculturalism. In the following paragraphs I wish to look specifically at the multicultural make-up of Australia's past and present by focusing on one particular migrant group, the Chinese. I have chosen the Chinese, because they have a long history in Australia, and as such they are useful historically as an illustration of how other groups than the British and the Irish were highly influential in giving shape to Australian identity.

In a more contemporary context the focus on the Chinese also grows out of my wish to place Australia in its geo-political sphere, both in contemporary terms, and historically. My reading questions the prevailing 'tyranny of distance' thesis fathered by Geoffrey Blainey,[199] which governs the view of many cultural historians. This thesis focuses on Australia's gradually successful overcoming of isolation, understood as isolation from the British Isles not as coming to terms with its geopolitical position. Instead the awkward in-betweenness of the space between Australia and Britain is re-produced as a cultural no-man's land, whose primary purpose is to confirm the lack of cultural trafficking between Australia and Asia.[200]

199. Blainey, of course, became famous for his criticism of Australia's multicultural turn in the 1980s and in particular for his opposition to Asian immigration.

200. Ignoring Asia has been central to the forging of a bond between Australia and Britain in colonial times. This 'sentimental attachment' has increasingly been replaced by a bond between Australia and 'the West', but Asia continues to be seen as an intransigent other best ignored

What I am arguing here is that there is a history of Australian-Asian links, which has been buried under the debris of an Australian orientalism, a history that since colonial times has existed alongside the cultural desires of seeing Australia as an extension of the British Isles. The duality of this historical legacy can be captured in the convict conviction that if they escaped across the Blue Mountains, China lay on the other side. So China existed in the colonial imagination, even if China was not necessarily seen as a desirable destination, but as a stepping-stone on the long road back to 'civilisation'.

Traditionally Australian nationalism has been cast in two different versions, a conservative one that emphasises the continued traits from a British legacy, and a nationalist one that stresses the radical/rebellious legacy of convictism, bushranging and gold-digging. Where one favours the successful transplantation of old British values to a new world, the other stresses the development of an anti-authoritarian sentiment, growing out of a resentment of old British values as undesirable for Australians. The conservative version tends to ignore the convicts (e.g. by focusing on the early decline in their share of the colonial population) and to dismiss the importance of convict uprisings, the Eureka Stockade and Ned Kelly (or at least as irrelevant to nation-forming), which are fundamental to the radical school. However, both schools accept the bush legend, and the legend of the Australian soldiers, as the decisive factors in consolidating a national identity. If the arguments by which this is reached are quite different, the two schools agree on the central elements in this process. The conservative stresses Anglo-Saxon 'gentleman' qualities enhanced by farming life in the bush, and the participation of Australian soldiers as a 'natural' part of its contribution to the common ideals of

---

except when a crisis erupts which is seen as a threat to Australia's territorial integrity or economic interests, or when an economic opportunity arises. Arguably little has changed in the general Australian attitude to Asia as 'teeming millions' with suspect agendas. Refugees coming into Australia continue to be cast in the mould of an invading army. One of the more interesting aspects of an otherwise appalling federal election campaign in 2001 was the competition over who could most effectively guarantee the impermeableness of the Australian coastline.

the British Empire. The radical school emphasises an anti-authoritarian legacy produced through the injustices committed by a British squattocracy, a British colonial Establishment and by ruthless British officers happily sacrificing the blood of dispensable colonials in both the Boer War and the First World War. But the two schools share the belief that the outcome of the nineteenth century bush experience and early twentieth century blood letting gave a definite and final shape to Australian identity. They are also similar in what they exclude from a national experience. Hence neither school deals in a satisfactory way with the displacement of Aborigines or the multicultural component in Australian history. As such both conservative and radical traditions trade in exclusivist, monocultural imaginings of Australia's past, which are then projected onto Australia's present, through a continuous obsession with received representations of national identity, such as the notion of the 'Aussie battler'.

The question then is what does the realisation that the Chinese have been in Australia virtually throughout its settlement history, and that there was extensive cultural traffic between Australia and China in the nineteenth century mean for the way we understand Australian identity? And furthermore, with the awareness of the long Chinese presence, how are we to conceive of the Chinese elements in the make-up of Australian culture? To begin to answer these questions requires an excavation of the Chinese presence and influence on Australian culture. This also includes the acknowledgement that the traits we recognise as typically Australian are not monoculturally derived, nor are they necessarily European in origin. The excavation of the Chinese impact on colonial Australia has been carried out by Eric Rolls in his monumental book, *Sojourners*. As an accumulation of evidence of the Chinese presence and influence in colonial Australia the book is unsurpassed, however, it falls short in deducing some deeper meaning of this presence. Hence while *Sojourners* expands dramatically the knowledge about the Chinese presence in colonial Australia, it offers little in terms of challenging existing patterns of representing Australian identity.

In spite of this, *Sojourners* remains a natural starting point due to its exhaustive treatment of the colonial Australian-

Chinese relations. Its explorations take place on three fronts; Chinese exploration and early contact history, Chinese immigrants in colonial Australia, and Australian- and European-Chinese relations in the nineteenth century. The parts that deal with migration and Australia focus on Chinese shepherds, golddiggers and other miners, gambling, opium and food, and finishes with the implementation of increasingly racist immigration laws as the nineteenth century draws to a close. Interestingly enough, Rolls's account reads like multicultural practice in reverse;[201] as preoccupations with a national identity begin to gather speed, Asian immigrants are increasingly harassed and driven out of the country. It is an irony with a somewhat bitter taste that what is often seen as the first instance of an Australian rebellion against colonial authority, the Eureka Stockade, also initiates the first organised racist campaign against the Chinese.

Yet what I find so disappointing about Rolls's account is that its wealth of accumulated knowledge is used for nothing but that, an endless stream of stories of Chinese lives and conditions in small pockets spread throughout settled Australia. Rich in detail on the diversity of occupations and descriptions of how they lived, how other colonials responded to them, it falls short in drawing any conclusions about general representations of the Chinese and about the impact they made on Australian culture. This critique is one that can indeed be widened in scope and be directed at historical representations of the Chinese in Australia generally. This point has been raised as an issue by Jan Ryan in her article 'Chinese Australian History', where she asks the question, 'why are historians not considering Chinese within discussions of Australia's identities?'[202] Ryan lets Sneja Gunew provide a tentative answer with her observation that '"consideration of one kind of history produces an even greater amnesia regarding other histories, including postwar migration histories", and that "Australians continue to seek national unities, coherent narratives of the nation."'[203] Yet, while I would agree with

201. See Rolls, pp. 456-57.

202. *Creating Australia*, p. 72.

203. Gunew quoted by Ryan in *Creating Australia*, p. 72.

Gunew's view, there is an essential part missing from her critique. For the problem is surely inherent to productions of nationalist histories, which by their nature include those, whose assimilation into the national narrative can override the contradictions such a move entails. Hence, it is no coincidence that the Australian pantheon of hero-material, from bushrangers to diggers, can include Germans, Italians and Danes, but not women, Aborigines or Chinese people, because their otherness cannot be included without undermining the ideological construction, which informs such monocultural representations. Such nationalist constructions are premised on an exclusivist nationalistic gaze that is male, white, and 'Anglo-Australian', and is contingent on selection and exclusion as Jon Stratton and Ien Ang have pointed out:

> The Australian type — sometimes spoken of as the 'Anglo-Australian race' — [which] was believed to be a new product of the multiplying British stock, the 'race' which, in the heyday of British imperialism and legitimated by the then immensely influential ideology of Social Darwinism, saw itself as superior to other 'races' and therefore possessing [sic] the duty and destiny to populate and civilise the rest of the world.[204]

To adopt a far more radical reading of a multicultural or a Chinese space in Australian culture is not only to recognise existing models of Australian identity's inability to satisfactorily integrate (as opposed to swallow up) migrant experiences, such as the Chinese. It strikes at the heart of the explanatory models themselves, exposing their essentially flawed premises and the racial legacy that is part and parcel of their historical origin. The point is not only to make visible what they exclude, but also to make apparent what they justify as a national experience Australians are supposed to identify with.

Australian models of national identity have not remained static. No static representation of national experience will survive in the long run, but the Australian models are essentially evolutionary, that is, they are gradually adjusted to incorporate women's histories, Aboriginal histories and migrant histories.

---

204. Jon Stratton and Ien Ang, 'Multicultural Imagined Communities', *Continuum*, vol. 8, no. 2 (1994), p. 130.

They are, as such, conservative and consensus seeking by nature, and both incapable of and unwilling to let themselves be challenged in a fundamental way. To meet the new cultural histories (new in the sense of being narrated, not in the sense of being) they have to be rethought in the light of the challenges posed by other emerging histories. It is not enough then to reformulate current ways of identifying Australian culture, it is necessary to trace those inconsistencies back to their origins. A post-colonial approach identifies such inconsistencies, because a post-colonial reading of Australian space juxtaposes the present concerns with their historical roots, and engages critically with contemporary readings of, for instance, a Chinese migrant space in an Australian context. How are such inconsistencies displayed? As Ryan argues in her article, contemporary historical representations of the Chinese are still somewhat at a loss, when it comes to considering the wider implications for Australian culture. The Chinese are still othered in relation to what is seen as important formative events in Australia's colonial history. Hence in the gold-digging period, which witnessed the first large-scale intake of Chinese migrants, Chinese are described mainly as victims of white abuse, as catalysts for latent racism. While there is no doubt that these events did take place, and such perceptions were widespread it is a reading that merely reproduces the Chinese as passive recipients of Australian racial hatred thus reproducing established categories of whites (settlers) and Chinese (migrants). Consider instead for a moment that the Chinese were abused of their legal rights as Australian colonials, a stance that presupposes the legitimacy of their claims to identify themselves with Australia/as Australians.[205] While it has become customary to look at daily life as a way of conveying historically contextualised living, such descriptions continue to exclude the Chinese, or look at them from an exclusively ethnographic angle.

If mainstream historical representations have been unable to de-exoticise the Chinese participation in giving shape to

205. Obviously, one could in the same way look at the 'white' side of the Eureka equation and argue that many of the golddiggers were first generation immigrants, which begs the question where the 'naturally' Australian anti-authoritarian behaviour is coming from?

Australian culture, there are illustrative examples in literature that show what forms a questioning of Australia's perceived origins of its identity can take. Literature by Chinese-Australian writers is fairly limited, yet there are examples of Chinese-Australian imaginings. The clearest case is perhaps Brian Castro's *Birds of Passage,* which in productive ways engages both with the meaning and the continuity of the Chinese presence in Australia. Castro achieves this through the split or doubling of the protagonist into a contemporary writer searching for identity by his reading and producing of the story of a Chinese migrant to the goldfields, or the arrival of a Chinese colonial. The historic character increasingly haunts the contemporary writer, who uses the story to retrace imaginatively his own ancestry back to the Chinese beginnings in colonial Australia. The novel also depicts Chinese interactions with other Australian colonials, relationships that in the novel exist alongside the racist abuse.

Yet the reversal of the gaze is not an activity exclusive to Chinese-Australians. One of the most interesting representations of Australia's Chinese legacy occurs in Alex Miller's novel, *The Ancestor Game*. Alex Miller challenges perceptions of Australia's past by continuously upsetting expectations about conventional representations through the juxtaposition of opposites, which becomes at once hilarious, tragic and subversive. Robert Sellick has described *The Ancestor Game* as dealing with characters whose principal characteristic is that they 'all suffer from a fundamental dislocation, as sense of exile, a radical displacement'. As Sellick furthermore points out with a quotation from the novel, 'Australia is identified as a land where "folk reside beyond the reach of history"; a place where "extraterritoriality is the status quo.... There is no nation here. Here the displaced are in place."'[206] Miller's novel is about ancestry, and its unpredictable but gripping nature. The novel opens with the return of the British born protagonist, Steven, who has returned from Australia to

206. Robert Sellick, 'Alex Miller: Games and Puzzles' in *A Talented Digger: Creations, Cameos and Essays in Honour of Anna Rutherford,* ed. by Hena Maes-Jelinek, Gordon Collier and Geoffrey V. Davis (Amsterdam: Rodopi, 1996), p. 443.

reconnect with his ancestral home in England, only to find it is a fruitless attempt at reconciliation, as are all such returns in the novel. Australia represents a new home, where one can reinvent oneself, but where the characters are also haunted by what they fled from. Exile and ancestry can be instrumental in the process of unravelling the nationalist anxiety to install a certain notion of reinventing or transplanting the ancestral self, a move which is essential to a nationalist imagining. However, while the two points I wish to pursue in my exploration of Miller's universe are somewhat related to this, I am also governed by my desire to place my reading in relation to the creation of a particular non-British-Australian space. To do this it is necessary to first briefly discuss Miller's presentation of a migrant Australian space, and, secondly, show how a particular passage illustrates the ways in which conventional nationalist representations of the bush ethos are subverted in *The Ancestor Game.*

The novel is set in England, China and Australia, yet, England merely operates as the narrator's frame for his personal trajectory between his ancestral home and his new displaced sense of belonging to Australia. The narrator presents an Australia which is simultaneously haunted by the anxious instalment of a transplanted cultural history which denies the history of displacement central to the idea of migrancy as a defining condition for Australians. The protagonist, if such a term is suitable for a novel engaging in endless reimaginings positioned in a blurry space between history and fiction, is Lang whose story is interwoven with those of a cohort of characters spread over a century of Chinese-Australian history. The novel doesn't deal overtly with Chinese-Australian relations, instead Chinese-Australian elements crop up at various points in the narrative where they disturb what otherwise appears to be a story about ancestry's hold on the migrant. In relation to my reading here, it is the intervention of different histories which belie the universal status granted to settlement narratives that is central.[207] In relation to the

207. Other ways of upsetting the conventional representational pattern of cultural reference points proliferate in the novel, such as the dismissal of Sidney Nolan's Australian iconography (seized upon by nationalists as typically Australian) as a 'regional vision located deep within the

significance of Chinese history in Australia one example is the Richmond house in Melbourne built by Feng in 1876, which becomes the focal point for a different story about the prolonged Chinese presence in Melbourne. The story, which unfolds, tells of cross-cultural interaction between Chinese and other migrants in Australia, but also of traffic between Melbourne and China, so Miller's story not only represents a different vision of Australia's past, it also problematises the tendency to see the Chinese history in Australia exclusively in terms of diaspora and isolation. Hence the historical vision Miller creates is not concerned with putting the neglected Chinese-Australian history on the map, but with showing that Australia's history has always been cross-cultural and as such shaped by a multicultural reality.[208] Presumably, this is one of the contributing factors which earned *The Ancestor Game* the label as a post-colonial novel in *The Oxford Literary History of Australia.*[209]

There is a central passage in the novel, which is a particularly apt illustration of how post-colonial narratives erupt through nationalist attempts at paving over difference, and instead suggest a far more multilayered reading of a quintessentially Australian experience. The passage describes the developing friendship, even mateship, between three characters Feng, Dorset and Patrick Nunan, who are shepherds near Ballarat in 1849, immediately prior to the discovery of gold in Australia. Several themes, which have a central role in narratives of Australian history, are introduced in this passage. Mateship formed in the bush in colonial Australia, frontier violence between whites and blacks, and the oncoming discovery of gold, which was to transform colonial Australia, particularly the colony of Victoria.

---

embrasures of a European tradition' (See Miller, pp. 7-8). An example of the many minor instances of Chinese-Australian associations is August Spiess's juxtaposition of Ballarat and Hangzhou (Miller, p. 275).

208. I use the term 'multicultural reality' here rather than 'multiculturalism', because of the latter term's unfortunate association with reification of cultures as discrete enclaves as a political strategy.

209. See *The Oxford Literary History* ed. by Bruce Bennett and Jennifer Strauss (Melbourne: Oxford University Press, 1998), pp. 252-53.

The three shepherds meet once a week to play Euchre, but when a Koorie kills a local white man, the local squatters form a search party with the black man Dorset as tracker. When they fail to locate the Koorie, they decide Dorset must be in league with the killer, and murder him. When Feng and Patrick find Dorset's body they decide to bury him, but wherever they dig they strike gold.

This preliminary sketchy, plot-orientated reading confirms conventional representations of colonial Australia. It presents themes, which are considered central to the formation of a particular Australian outlook, either in the conservative form of transplanted British values, or in accordance with the radical tradition which emphasises egalitarian and anti-authoritarian values and attitudes. However, a closer perusal of the passage quickly reveals that Miller's game here is a different one. First of all the narrator is a blind Chinese storyteller, which questions the implicit notion of Australians telling the national stories, while simultaneously confirming the Australian tradition of spinning a yarn. Secondly, as their names suggest, the three characters are not the conventional representative figures suitable for British-Australian transplantations of kiplingsque ideals into the Australian bush; an Irishman, a Chinese who has lost his ancestry, and an Aborigine who is clueless in the bush, because he has been raised in aristocratic circles in England. Importantly, this makes him not so much an Aboriginal mimic of a white man, as the embodiment of upper-class English values. The theme Miller pursues here is the double position of the exile as simultaneously freedom and imprisonment, through the incongruous material he presents for the narration of an Australian legend.

Links are created between the characters in a fashion that both confirms Australia's status as a place for newcomers, while it questions the legacy of these newcomers as necessarily British-Australian. This point is illustrated by Miller's description of the link between the incongruously ancestor-less Feng and tribe-less Dorset:

> As with Feng, Dorset possessed only one name. Which seemed to be a common condition among those who had become severed from their tribes. He sprang from a

> proud nation, he claimed, and quite as ancient as the Han.[210]

Miller's combination of an unconventional use of conventional narrations of Australian themes, easily recognised from the bush ethos, continues as a running commentary, which ironically exposes the mythology, which inhabits the Australian bush ethos:

> They communicated in a language of their own invention. They dug about in likely corners of Gaelic and Fukienese and English for this and that part of speech, and constructed a lingo comprehensible only to themselves.... They became masters of linguistic make-do.[211]

The bush-craftmanship in their linguistic adaptability gives voice to a far more multicultural vision than the one, which is generally allowed in Australian colonial representations.[212] The question arises, from the importance granted to the way in which colonial (hi)story is told, who is in fact telling Miller's story, the blind storyteller or Miller himself? The blind storyteller operates as a displacement of the conventional narrator, through which the reader's attention is brought to the peculiarity of the passage narrated, which on a grander scale exposes the conventionality of nationalist representations. For whilst drawing attention to the constructedness of his narrative, Miller's narration works inside a frame that is recognisably historical, as the narrator points out: 'The facts are important. The shaping spirit of the story is not my own'.[213] Presumably the narrator is the blind Chinese storyteller, but the forces overriding his story (dictating the frame) are the facts of history, *i.e.* dispossession and gold discovery. Hence

---

210. Miller, p. 221.

211. Miller, p. 222.

212. Although Miller is primarily spinning a yarn, he is also drawing attention to the multicultural reality of colonial Australia. It is worth remembering that the most famous celebration of the bush myth, *Waltzing Matilda*, contains Aboriginal creolised words, but also that the word Matilda, was probably brought by German migrants from South Australia to the gold fields. Yet, the song has been hailed and claimed for a version of colonial Australia that disregards any share of colonials from other backgrounds in the particular shape that colonial sentiment took.

213. Miller, p. 223.

the difference lies in the narration, the choice of angle, choice of protagonist, for the frame in which they operate is demarcated by colonial history. Miller's preoccupation with colonial history can be seen through his almost obsessive description of historical change that is where, as he describes it, history enters and lays claim to the lives of the characters. Here where Feng realises the ominous nature of the visit by the squatters, who have come to look for Dorset to use him as a tracker:

> The world *had* changed. He had understood at the moment of waking that he was no longer in the place where he had gone to sleep. And he had understood, also, that there could be no regaining that former place. He knew there could be no going back to it. He had closed his eyes and a catalyst had been slipped into the mix of their new society and had caused this group of men to separate out and to form a single body united by a common identity and a common purpose. While he'd slept something had awoken in these mounted men the knowledge that they were of the same tribe. Some event had threatened their species and had stirred within them the latent memory of ancestral bonds, and, in becoming the familiars of each other, they had become strangers to him. Feng knew all this....[214]

The change is the break-down of the hybrid space inhabited by the three shepherds through the intrusion of colonial reality. What replaces this hybrid space is a monocultural drive to put everyone in their 'proper tribal' context, whether they have abandoned it or not (which both Feng and Dorset have), and regardless of whether the concept of tribe has ceased to be meaningful to them:

> [Dorset] understood that the essence of freedom is in dislocation from one's origins, that freedom is to be judged for oneself and not for one's tribe. He understood that freedom is identity for the individual. And, as he rode about the place in his futile search for the murderer, he did not expect this to change suddenly.[215]

214. Miller, p. 225.

215. Miller, p. 227.

The squatters on the other hand insist on tribal connections as the defining quality, and the failure to live up to their tribal expectations, constitutes a betrayal of their image, which they are dependent upon to justify their own situation. Beneath their insistence on tribal identification of selves and others lurks the anxious realisation that other alternative readings of Australian space, beyond the reach of a transplanted British identity, will threaten the legitimacy they have established on an exclusively monocultural identification of colonial Australian space. It is this, which leads them to pursue the idea of tribal identification beyond any meaningful boundary:

> And so they made a mistake; a true error of judgement. For they judged Dorset not as a man like themselves, not as a free man, but as the son of his ancestors. They had not understood that Dorset, the individual, was unable to read the text of the landscape of his forebears. They believed in his innate ability to read it. And they concluded, therefore, that he was misleading them.[216]

This passage does suggest a case of normal relations suspended, that is, usually amicable relations are driven away by a circumscribed understanding of 'intertribal' relations, but the passage also shows that the level of tolerance is contingent on the nature of the white occupation. Their dispossession of Aborigines leads them to make irrational assessment, their actions are governed by their own latent paranoia:

> The poor quality of their judgement concerning Dorset's relation to his ancestors, based as it was on an assumption of innate differences and on guilt and a certain superstitious fear of losing what they had gained by illicit means, misled them. It offered them uncertainty and fed their paranoia, and it made them draw more closely together to find comfort and support in each other.
>
> And in doing this they forfeited their freedom to make judgements as individuals and they became a tribe themselves, bound by a common ancestral imperative.[217]

216. Miller, p. 229.
217. Miller, p. 229.

Miller's use of tribalism as a bond used to exclude others is placed in a direct historical context here, but has interesting repercussions for the later construction of nationalist myths, which are premised precisely on the idea of tribalism. In Miller's reading they act against their better judgement, they fail to use rational judgement, favouring instead an emotional response, emphasising rash certainties in response to their own doubts concerning the nature of their enterprise. Hence, the point is that though gaps are allowed to emerge in the colonialist attempts at resurfacing the colonial space, such gaps are closed up at the moment of conflict. Arguably conflict leads to sacrifice which in turn feeds into constructions of national identity, which in Australian nationalist narratives are mirrored by the preferred legend material of convicts (sacrifice of freedom and blood), bushrangers and golddiggers (rebellion against intrinsically alien and repressive authority), explorers (death sacrifice for the greater good of all Australians, that is, opening up the country) and soldiers (sacrifice in a battle that gave Australia maturity as a nation). Miller's narrative challenges both the material from which myths such as these are built, but also the nature of them. Hence while Dorset is sacrificed in what could be seen as an illustration of the general persecution of Aborigines, his peculiar status precludes such a finding, and as a broader questioning of the point in such sacrifices, the burial of Dorset becomes an ironic gesture, where the wrongly treated are compensated in a moment of supreme irony:

> In the days and weeks that followed they tried the ground all-round the lonely spot where Dorset lay, but they could not find a place to put him. Wherever they opened the earth they discovered gold. Dorset's motherland resisted his interment. She refused to take him back. There was to be no reconciliation between them. She offered the inducement of her gold rather than receive him to her bosom. He had declared himself free and free he would remain.[218]

Belonging and unbelonging is also a theme that is central to the poetry of the Chinese-born poet, Ouyang Yu. But where

218. Miller, p. 234.

Miller's vision questions the nature of what is, after all, a construction of belonging and unbelonging, Yu's poetry comes with the acute awareness of being in both camps at the same time. Although there are moments of freedom in Yu's poetry, the poet is always ultimately claimed by either his new or old country. This is brought out with immediate clarity in his first published collection of poetry, *Moon Over Melbourne*.[219] In 'Song for an Exile in Australia' he writes, 'I feel doubly alienated/the death of the old world has such weird attractions/while the light of the new world has somehow darkened' (p. 15). For Yu exile is primarily a sense of loss, even at moments which may also hold a liberating potential:

> in a season without languages in Australia
> I have lost my weight in undeveloped no-person's land
> like a wild devil roaming
> I sow my language into the alien soil
> where it sends forth strange flowers that no one recognises
> and all of a sudden I find my tongue held
> between two languages like a vice (p. 15)

The feeling of being held by the old country develops at times into paranoia, 'wherever you go/china follows you/like a shadow/its ancientness/recast in australia' (p. 36). The sense of entrapment comes to the poet in different ways; in relation to China it is a feeling of not being able to escape, in a similar way to Miller's idea of ancestry as a denial of individual freedom. In relation to Australia it is the continued refused acceptance that haunts the poet. This is most clearly voiced in the aptly titled poem 'Fuck you, Australia', which is a critique of Australian racist attitudes to Chinese. Interestingly, the imagery in this poem blends the historical with the contemporary; 'digging for gold in your cheap sunshine/...you thought in your heart of hearts that we were bad/not fit to share your continent' (p. 79), which shows the continuity of the Chinese migrant's predicament, borne out by the list of Australian attitudes that has remained more or less unchanged since the arrival of the Chinese on the goldfields. If the above

---

219. Ouyang Yu, *Moon Over Melbourne and Other Poems* (Melbourne: Papyrus Publishing, 1995). All subsequent quotations are from this collection and page references are included in the text.

tends towards an outline of abuse and victimisation, Yu also suggests an outlet for agency for the migrant. The poem finishes with the, at least in this context, optimistic line 'that I'd come back one day to pick up an australian woman/as my tenth concubine' (p. 79). But agency is not the only departure from the abusive history of Chinese migrants. Irony, is perhaps the most effective countermeasure, because it operates as a subversive stratum, that both exposes white racist attitudes and draws attention to the migrant's own participation in some of the ritualistic exchanges of abuse. Hence the poem 'Fuck you, Australia' carries the subtitle 'from a penniless gambler', drawing attention to the Chinese predilection for gambling, as well as suggesting the migrant has and is spent and forced to return to China, after having given up being accepted by the new country.

Behind the themes of racist abuse, double exile and alienation lies the concept of cultural translation. Yu has dedicated two poems specifically to this concept, namely 'Interview with Yu' and 'Translating Myself'. In the former poem, Yu is being interviewed and after being branded with the customary ethnicity label he is asked the customary question 'but why do you write in english' (p. 42), hence immediately a gap is established between identity and preferred mode of communication, which is countered later in the exchange 'sorry can i ask why do you not write in chinese/ your own language/i do not own a language' (p. 43). If this exchange betrays the preconceived ideas of the interviewer, the prejudice entailed by the question becomes even more exposed in the passage, where Yu is asked about his view on the Chinese migrants:

> all traitors
> really
> all want to renounce their nationality
> and become australian citizens
> good on them
> can't you let me finish my words decently
> sorry
> all want to renounce their nationality
> and become australian citizens
> before going back to their country of origin

and enjoy the best of both worlds
because they are australian in china and chinese in australia (p. 44)

The passage shows the centrality of commitment as opposed to convenience that runs through Yu's poetry, as a response to being acutely aware of otherness as the 'inalienable' predicament of the migrant.

In 'Translating Myself' Yu takes a more linguistic departure in his assessment of relating to two very different cultures at the same time. The poem recounts translation as a moment of doubt, even loss and alienation:

translating myself is a problem
I mean how can I turn myself into another language
without surrendering myself
without betraying myself
without forgetting myself
without forgiving myself
without even losing myself in a different con/text (p. 82)

The doubts expressed by Yu here articulates the fear of losing one's roots in the act of translating oneself culturally from a Chinese context to an Australian one. Later, however, this anxiety is replaced by a feeling of translation not as a process of losing, but of gaining a duality, a space outside the confinement of a particular culture, where the gain comes from the dialogue initiated between the two halves of the poet's identity:

or is this body of mine really two bodies
one English
the other Chinese
translating myself is but re/creating
myself with languages or bodies
a discourse between two knowing halves
or wholes
each the interpreter of the other (p. 82)

The potential of this dialogue is clear from Yu's tentative suggestion that the two contexts may provide at least 'knowing halves' and possibly even 'wholes', which productively engage in a process of mutual explication.

What is then to be uncovered from such an exchange that may not surface from a mono-linguistic/-cultural investigation Yu casts in the personal realisation of what is concealed in languages, via the entrance of an(other) language:

> I translate myself
> from Chinese into English
> disappear into appearance of
> another existence looking back across
> the barrier of tied tongues
> at the concealed image of the other body (p. 83)

I would like to move outside the obvious benefits of the self-referentiality to the poet split between two cultures, and how such a process may develop into a healing exercise through a reconciliation between othered selves, to consider what Yu's poetry may offer at a larger level with regards to envisioning a multicultural Australia.

The exposure of bigotry is the most immediately recognisable aim in Yu's poetry, also because it is formulated in unequivocal language. There are few redeeming features to be found in racists attitudes and stereotypes. Yet, prejudice as a built-in self-critique of the Chinese migrant's dismissive perceptions of Australia is an important phenomenon as well. Here Yu's critique takes two departures, one that is aimed at the wealthy Chinese migrants thinking Australia is another place to colonise in economic terms, and another which criticises the Chinese for not investing culturally in Australia. In both instances Yu presents an image of migrants who have no eyes for the culture that is there but only for the degree to which it can be plundered. This attitude has been enhanced through the Australian business migration scheme, which allows moneyed Asians to jump the migration queue, and pay their way into the country.

There is no easy reconciliation in Yu's poetry between the severed cultural halves, whether they are made up by personal splits, or more generally by cultural differences. Multiculturalism is an agonising process that has no alternative, except for monocultural isolation. A reading of multiculturalism that recurs often in the Australian debate, and one that is perhaps a consequence of the urgency to find positive identification models which do not correspond to multicultural reality. Hence one of the arguments being used draws attention to the fact that certain white groups are more in need of support than some segments of the migrant community, if Australia is to avoid facing an increasingly polarised community. With the onslaught of globalisation the solidarity of the Australian society will be placed under increasing stress. This will also be a test of the degree to which a multicultural perspective has become integral to perceptions of Australian identity.

Conclusion

Multiculturalism has come under a great deal of flak in recent years. At times it has been outwardly dismissed as an ideological strategy aimed at containing the racialised other through strategic containment, e.g. folkloric inclusion at the cost of excluding processes of real differential treatment. Its categorisations of cultures are seen as having participated in forming strategic conservative enclaves, and creating alliances between a conservative political Establishment and an equally conservative led 'ethnic' Establishment. One of the earliest books which sought to carve out a multicultural history of Australia is *Mistaken Identity*, written by Stephen Castles, Mary Kalantzis, Bill Cope and Michael Morrisey in 1988. The collective from Wollongong University's Centre for Multicultural Studies were less concerned with what might be characteristic of an Australian multicultural practice and outlook. However, they were aware of the pitfalls of uncritically embracing the often obsessive modernity that drives multiculturalism as an ideology. This balancing between the enabling and disabling characteristics of multiculturalism is set out in two central paragraphs worth quoting at length here:

> Multiculturalism is progressive because it attempts to define the nation in non-nationalistic, non-ethnocentric terms. It is regressive because in some of its guises it often trivializes more serious social issues of inequality, founded in socio-economic structures, gender relations and structural racism. Its affirmative celebration of being colourfully different is a frequent cloak for deep-seated racism, for the continuing exclusion of Aborigines from Australian society, for the hardships of immigration, for the virtual exclusion of women from structures of economic and political power. Multiculturalism is

> regressive for a second reason: it does not question the need to define the nation and to draw boundaries of inclusion and exclusion. By celebrating diversity within the nation, it reaffirms, even if often only in a perfunctory way, the need for a national cohesion which is more than that of face-to-face community and less than that of all humanity. The step beyond multiculturalism is the transcending of national identity, the denial of its necessity, the recognition that through the crisis of modernity we are now all in the same boat — economically, ecologically and politically. Human identity must become transnational.[220]

The passage is central for its espousal of a very clearly defined critical stance, a departure for the dismantling of the national imaginary. That departure, which is here defined as 'transnational' can assume many different guises, I think, depending on the particular context it is placed in. In what ways for example does transnationalism make room for the necessarily separate space inside which Aborigines and Torres Strait Islanders can articulate a sense of identity that is not merely reduced to the competitive field of other minorities? How does, if it is supposed to do so, transnationalism address the unequal position both of minorities *vis-à-vis* the majority, but also *vis-à-vis* each other? I agree with the writers when they argue for the need to dismantle the national imaginary as that which has been championed as guaranteeing a social cohesiveness, when it has in fact operated as a divisive device aimed at perpetuating the privileged position of the Anglo-Irish Australians. However, when it comes to putting something instead that provides a transnational solidarity, it is difficult to see what forms the basis of this solidarity other than the nation's space, at least as long as that remains the provider of the means for the political-social community.

The model of multiculturalism, here in its Australian form, has offered a new departure for conceptualising an Australian identity away from the conventional settler narrative of

220. Stephen Castles, Bill Cope, Mary Kalantzis and Michael Morrissey, *Mistaken Identity: Multiculturalism and the Demise of Nationalism in Australia* (Sydney: Pluto Press, 1988), p. 13.

Australian origins deriving from British-Irish stock, away from the representation of physical and psychological transplantation. However, multiculturalism has also been haunted by a progressivist tale of minorities whose successful incorporation into Australian overrides the need to fundamentally revise the settlement narrative. Furthermore, multicultural history writing has failed to sufficiently well address the issue that multiculturalism as a political platform has been constructed on the premise that it is virtually cost-free for the already privileged majority of Australians. The obsessive modernity discourse which informs multiculturalism stems from a reluctance to come to terms both with the colonial legacy of racist motivated violence and exclusionary mechanisms put in operation against Asian migrants and indigenous Australians. Modernity discourse centres on itself as the solution to cultural stalemates, irreconcilable difference is replaced with a celebration of diversity and an indeterminacy of identity. However, until the issues which have been brought into being by colonialism and which continue to live on in displaced form in the neo-colonialism of Anglo-Irish privileges are adequately dealt with and incorporated into conceptualisations of what Australian identity has been based on in the past, how can anyone really believe in a genuinely new departure. In particular because so many of those problems which originated in colonial Australia live on in, even only at times, displaced forms. The current Prime Minister is on record for (a) speaking against Asian immigration (albeit this was in the 1980s, no serious observer would believe he has really changed his views),[221] (b) refusing to apologise for dehumanising practices carried out against Aboriginal children up until the 1970s, (c) putting as many obstacles in the way for Aboriginal land rights claims as possible, (d) criminalising what is internationally recognised as a legitimate right for people to seek political asylum and (e) when refugees do manage to arrive to place them in concentration camp style confinement beyond reach of the media, (f) managing to alienate Australia's relations with most of its Southeast Asian

221. See Ien Ang, *On Not Speaking Chinese* (London: Routledge, 2001), p. 110.

neighbourhood and finally (g) seeking to maximise the profits from the Timor Gap against the internationally recognised rights of the now independent East Timor.

This, I realise, reads as a diatribe against the Howard government, however it has fully earned this critique through some really hard work. Yet, it is also a wider indictment of the Australian political Establishment, for there seems to be little anyone has to offer in terms of alternatives. How different is this situation not to a decade ago, when none of these issues featured in this dismal way on the Australian political agenda, even in its also then nationalistic preoccupation? Transnationalism may sound like a genuine new departure, in particular if it is meant to be a cross-cultural domestic platform, and I also hasten to add that the political climate in which *Mistaken Identity* was written was far more optimistic. However, what is sorely needed before any such departure can be embarked upon is a critical examination of the operations and pressures which the nationalist imagery in all its operations (through education, the media, the political system etc.) can bring to bear on all the marginalised groups in the Australian society.

REFERENCES

Ang, Ien, *On Not Speaking Chinese: Living Between Asia and the World* (London: Routledge, 2001).

Broinowsky, Alison, *The Yellow Lady: Australian Impressions of Asia* (Melbourne: Oxford U.P., 1992).

Castro, Brian, *Birds of Passage* (Sydney: Allen & Unwin, 1983).

Castro, Brian, *Writing Asia and Autobiography: Two Lectures* (Canberra: University College, Australian Defence Force Academy, 1995), pp. 1-21.

Cushman, J.W., 'A "colonial casualty": The Chinese Community in Australian Historiography', *Asian Studies of Australia*, vol. 7, no. 3.

Gunew, Sneja, 'Denaturalizing cultural nationalisms: multicultural readings of "Australia"' in *Nation and Narration*, ed. by Homi Bhabha (London: Routledge, 1990).

Gunew, Sneja and Kateryna O. Longley (eds), *Striking Chords: Multicultural Literary Representations* (Sydney: Allen & Unwin, 1992).

Hamilton, Annette, 'Fear and Desire: Aborigines, Asians and the National Imaginary', in *Australian Cultural History (Australian Perceptions of Asia)*, 9 (1990), pp. 14-35.

Jose, Nicholas, *Chinese Whispers: Cultural Essays* (Kent Town, S.A.: Wakefield Press, 1995).

Miller, Alex, *The Ancestor Game* (Ringwood: Penguin, 1992).

Mistaken Identity: Multiculturalism and the Demise of Nationalism in Australia, Stephen Castles, Bill Cope, Mary Kalantzis and Michael Morrissey (Leichhardt: Pluto Press, 1988).

Palfreeman, A.C., *The Administration of the White Australia Policy* (Melbourne: Melbourne University Press, 1967).

Rolls, Eric, *Sojourners: Flowers and the Wide Sea* (St. Lucia: University of Queensland Press, 1992).

Ryan, Jan, 'Chinese Australian History' in *Creating Australia: Changing Australian History* ed. by Wayne Hudson and Geoffrey Bolton (St. Leonards: Allen & Unwin, 1997).

Sellick, Robert, 'Alex Miller: Games and Puzzles' in *A Talented Digger: Creations, Cameos and Essays in Honour of Anna Rutherford,* ed. by Hena Maes-Jelinek, Gordon Collier and Geoffrey V. Davis (Amsterdam: Rodopi, 1996), pp. 443-48.

Stratton, Jon and Ien Ang, 'Multicultural Imagined Communities', *Continuum,* vol. 8, no. 2 (1994).

The Oxford Literary History ed. by Bruce Bennett and Jennifer Strauss (Melbourne: Oxford University Press, 1998).

Yu, Ouyang, *Moon Over Melbourne* (Upper Ferntree Gully: Papyrus Publishing, 1995).

Yu, Ouyang, *Songs of the Last Chinese Poet* (Sydney: Wild Peony, 1997).